ALASKA IC

First Edition

Kelsey Gray, Burrell Nickeson & Chris Lindsey

ISBN: 978-1-7327355-1-4

Printed in China through
Alaska Print Brokers, Anchorage, Alaska
Book design: Kelsey Gray, Reinventing the Nomad Publishing
Cover artwork by Sarah K. Glaser, the photo used as
inspiration can be found on page 188.

Published by
Reinventing the Nomad
Anchorage, Alaska

This book is available for order online:
alaskaiceclimbing.com & climbak.com

Warning!

Climbing is an inherently dangerous sport in which severe injuries or death may occur. Relying on the information in this book may increase the danger.

When climbing, you can only rely on your skill, training, experience, and conditioning. If you have any doubts as to your ability to safely climb any route in this guide, do not try it.

This book is neither a professional climbing instructor nor a substitute for one. It is not an instructional book; do not use it as one. It contains information that is nothing more than a compilation of opinions about climbing in Alaska. These opinions are neither facts nor promises. Treat the information as opinions and nothing more. Do not substitute these opinions for your own common sense and experience.

Assumption of Risk

There may be errors in this book resulting from the mistakes of the authors and/or the people with whom they consulted. The information was gathered from a variety of sources, which may not have been independently verified. Those who provided the information may have made mistakes in their descriptions. The authors may have made mistakes in their conveyance of the information in this book. **The authors cannot, therefore, guarantee the correctness of any of the information contained in this book.** The topographical maps, photo-diagrams, difficulty ratings, protection ratings, approach and/or descent information, suggestions about equipment, and other matters may be incorrect or misleading. Fixed protection may be absent, unreliable, or misplaced. **You must keep in mind that the information in this book may be erroneous, so use your own judgment when choosing, approaching, climbing, or descending from a route described in this book.**

DO NOT USE THIS BOOK UNLESS YOU [AND YOUR ESTATE] PROMISE NEVER TO TRY TO SUE US IF YOU GET HURT OR KILLED.

Disclaimer of Warranties

THE AUTHORS AND PUBLISHER WARN THAT THIS BOOK CONTAINS ONLY THE AUTHOR'S OPINIONS ON THE SUBJECTS DISCUSSED. WE MAKE NO OTHER WARRANTIES EXPRESSED OR IMPLIED, OF MERCHANTABILITY, FITNESS FOR PURPOSE, OR OTHERWISE, AND IN THE EVENT, OUR LIABILITY FOR BREACH OF ANY WARRANTY OR CONTRACT WITH RESPECT TO THE CONTENT OF THIS BOOK IS LIMITED TO THE PURCHASE PRICE OF THE BOOK. WE FURTHER LIMIT TO SUCH PURCHASE PRICE OUR LIABILITY ON ACCOUNT OF ANY KIND OF NEGLIGENT BEHAVIOR WHATSOEVER ON OUR PART WITH RESPECT TO THE CONTENTS OF THIS BOOK.

Travis Mcalpine starting Sword and the Stone with Josh Pickle on belay, the pillar was nearly at full ice strength turning this original mixed line into an ice route

CONTENTS

THE QUICK AND DIRTY

Getting to Alaska: Getting to Alaska is going to be straightforward for most of the users of this book. You either live here or you're going to fly in. While there may be some who drive up during the winter, it is not the ideal method. If you drove nonstop from Seattle to Anchorage, it would take you about 40 hours in good conditions. That doesn't include sleeping time. There are several airlines that service Alaska's main airports, including Anchorage and Fairbanks. A quick check of your favorite travel websites should give you an idea of options and ticket prices, but prices will likely vary between $100 and $300 from Seattle during the winter months. If you plan on going to other areas of the state, such as Valdez or Seward, the price of flying can go up significantly and it is usually worth it to just rent a car and drive there yourself.

Staying: Once you arrive there are plenty of places to stay. Hostels exist (although some are not desirable) and it is best to read online reviews of any place you plan on staying. Anchorage also has the usual hotels, such as Sheraton, Hilton, ect... There are plenty of bed & breakfast type accommodations, as well as lodges, and we highly recommend

staying at local companies to support Alaskan businesses. Anchorage is a good base camp for several areas in this book although it can really help to stay closer to the climbing areas. Alaska gets a limited amount of sun during the winter, with the shorter days averaging about 4-5 hours of total sunlight near Anchorage. If you drive from Anchorage to Caribou Creek, it will take about 2 hours each way and this can eat up daylight time quickly.

Renting a Car: Renting a car in Alaska can be a good idea. Transportation around Anchorage exists but you'll spend so much time waiting you're probably better off just walking to your destination. Beyond Anchorage transportation becomes immediately limited. Without a rental car to get outside Anchorage even climbing on the Seward Highway is difficult and would cost a fortune to use a cab or Uber. Midnight Sun is a good option if you use a local car company. We also have the larger companies such as Hertz, Budget, and Enterprise. Many of the major car companies can be picked up at the airport. Alaska 4x4 Rentals can also be found in the North Terminal of Ted Stevens International Airport, they have many high quality off-road vehicles at a decent winter price. Their Jeep Wranglers, if conditions were right, could get you to Friday Creek as easy as many other areas. In the 90's Charlies Sassara once drove his Suburban to the mouth of Friday Creek. If you decide to rent an economy or midsize car, be aware that your travel may be limited depending on road conditions. During a heavy snowfall, Anchorage can get several feet of snow in a few days. It is highly suggested that you get a vehicle with studs, or at the least an all wheel drive vehicle with winter tires. Keep in mind that schools in Anchorage have been closed more for icy roads than for snow. The roads are slick in Alaska. Chains can be nice to have if you get stuck but are not normally used to drive around on except for extreme circumstances, such as steep hills off the main roads.

5

WEATHER

The weather in Alaska is highly variable and can change daily. The chart below is meant to give an overall idea on what could be the best time to climb in each area. Each bar is a representation of when you could expect there to be ice in the area, when it is most often in season, and the time the ice is usually melted out. The chart also takes into account access. For example, Boulder Creek will likely freeze long before December but access can be difficult as the river also needs to freeze to facilitate any kind of speedy approach. A cold snap early or late in the year will also quickly skew this chart and some areas could see first ice around September if the conditions are right. Likewise, areas such as Portage and the Seward Highway may hit warm spells in January. The best time to visit Alaska for ice climbing is from December until February when the cold temperatures are more consistent and most areas are accessible.

AREA	SEP	OCT	NOV	DEC	JAN	FEB	MAR	APR	MAY
Boulder Creek									
Caribou Creek									
Dragonfly Creek									
Eagle River									
Eklutna Canyon									
Eklutna Glacier									
Fish Hatchery									
Fox Creek									
Friday Creek									
Glacier Creek									
Glen Alps									
Gravel Creek									
Hatcher Pass									
Homer									
Hunter Creek									
Jack River									
Keystone Canyon									
Knik Gorge									
Mineral Creek									
Nabesna									
Pioneer Peak									
Portage Valley									
Purinton Creek									
Seward Highway									
Tonsina Creek									
Victor Creek									
Whittier									

ICONS

The icons that we use in the book are suggestions. They are not to be taken as gospel and due to legal access issues, snowfall, climate change, can vary from season to season. It is best to check multiple sources for information on accessing ice climbing areas and the legality behind using snowmachines, ATVs, or even fatbikes.

 Number of Routes

The number of routes located within a specific area.

 Avalanche

Avalanches are a real possibility; know the conditions before approaching. What does it mean to "know the conditions"? You should take an avalanche safety course, check all online weather sites, such as Chugach National Forest Avalanche Information Center (http://www.cnfaic.org/) and become knowledgeable in avalanche safety.

 Snowmachine

Snowmachine use is recommended in reducing approach time. Access can be restricted during specific times of the year; it is your responsibility to check any access issues.

 ATVs

ATVs are recommended due to vehicular restrictions or terrain not ideal for snowmachines. It is your responsibility to check on access issues and timing.

 Fatbike

Fatbikes are a newer trend that can reduce approach times and effort. Access is generally open for most areas.

 Skiing

Skiing can greatly reduce approach times and effort needed to approach the climbs.

 Road Hazards

This icon is specifically for the Seward Highway and indicates that there is a real danger of being struck by a vehicle while climbing or belaying.

 Boat

There are some areas that may require a boat during specific times of the year. E.g. *Hands Across* the Water at Portage Glacier. If the lake is not frozen then this route requires a trip across in a boat.

X-DREAM

The X-Dream is the only ice tool designed to adapt to every kind of technical alpine terrain. We do it with a patented handle that allows the climber to switch the angle from ice to dry. With four pick configurations, two handle options and new head weights for cold and brittle ice, the X-Dream is truly the most versatile ice tool on the market. Best of all, it features the perfectly balanced swing that Cassin tools are known for, making every move more secure.

camp-usa.com/outdoor

RATINGS BREAKDOWN

Water Ice Rating

Water ice (WI) is not a static medium like rock, which makes it sometimes difficult to give a route a specific rating. Depending on the time of season, time of day, or which part of an icefall is climbed, the ice conditions can vary, sometimes significantly. To add additional confusion, the use of (+) and (-) may be added to the end of the WI numeral rating system to define a route as being slightly harder (+) or slightly easier (-). For example, a WI3+ will be considered slightly harder than a WI3, but may not be as difficult as a WI4-. That said, for this book, the applied ratings should be assumed when the route is in its most common condition.

Zachary Newmark on Pilsner Pillar at the Beer Climbs, Pioneer Peak during the University of Alaska Anchorage's ice climbing course (Courtesy Serina Marie)

WI1 - A walkup that requires only crampons to ascend.

WI2 - The ice is about 65 degrees and requires crampons and the use of at least one ice tool. Routes of this rating are ideal for those just learning how to climb ice.

WI3 - A sustained route of approximately 75 degrees with occasional vertical steps of no more than 10 meters. Protection is typically considered good throughout the route.

WI4 - Routes at approximately 75-85 degrees with vertical steps slightly greater than 10 meters. Rests can be minimal so strength and stamina start becoming a factor. Protection is still considered good.

WI5 - Routes are now vertical or near vertical for 20 meters or greater. Rests are minimal and climbing is strenuous and technical. Protection is decent. This rating can also define ice that is good, but very thin.

WI6 - Bring a clear head as routes in this category are completely vertical or overhanging with no rests. Movements are highly technical and require some creativity. Strength, balance and stamina are necessary to ascend. Protection is less available.

WI7 - Uncommon. Ice is completely overhanging and may be considered dangerous. Protection is minimal to none. Climbing movements may be delicate and require a high degree of precision and creativity. Climbing in this realm requires extreme strength and stamina.

ABOUT THE AUTHORS

(Courtesy John Borland)

Kelsey Gray

Kelsey loves to climb rocks. The problem is he's in Alaska where the rocks are covered by an often thin veneer of water in its solid state. This means he has to either suffer in cold temperatures climbing rock or move on to the ice and become one with the cold. It also has something to do with an obsession that started years ago and causes him to count bolts on faraway obscure climbs in foreign countries and carry a large camera deep into dark ice-filled canyons, always looking for the next opportunity. He spends his time in Alaska teaching ice and rock climbing at the University of Alaska Anchorage and writing guidebooks, such as this one, for the good of humanity. Other books he's written are the Alaska Rock Climbing Guide, Alaska Bouldering Guide (co-author, and let's face it, mostly design), Just Us Down Here, and Found Wandering, as well as publishing the Alaska Roadside Angler's Guide.

Burrell Nickeson

With absolutely no climbing experience, Burrell moved from Wyoming to Alaska in 1997 with a desire to spend time in the outdoors. A couple years later, some friends took him ice climbing and it wasn't long after he became hooked on the sport. In the early 2000's, Burrell and Chris Lindsey created Alaskaiceclimbing.com, a free-to-the-public online ice climbing guide, which has since grown to include more than 300 ice routes. As of this book he is taking a hiatus from ice climbing in order to spend more time skiing with his daughter, Jihyeon.

Chris Lindsey

20 years ago Chris left the comfortable rock crags of Texas and Mexico in search of riches and adventure in the Last Frontier. Upon arrival, it was immediately clear that the vast wilderness of Alaska provided climbing opportunities that were unquenchable. Knowledge of the best areas was scant, so beta was paramount. Luckily, he met locals like Eddie Phay early on that were willing to share their local expertise. Eddie's immediate willingness to show him the way to hidden Seward Highway rock cliffs left an indelible mark. It was clear that Arctic winters also provided consistent climbing opportunities up frozen waterfalls. The ice in this vast state was plentiful but once again he found the information was not. Suffering took on a whole new meaning while searching for untouched vertical treasures hiding around the next ridge in sub-zero temperatures. So in 2005, after years of backcountry exploration, Burrell and Chris started Alaskaiceclimbing.com. The goal was clear, to document the location and history of ice climbing so that others would benefit, a mantra kept with the publishing of this guide.

(Courtesy Paul Guzenski)

V-Threads: The Abalakov Thread (V-Thread for short) is the gold standard for abseiling ice climbs. This method was devised by Vitaly Abalakov, the Russian climber who also invented the first curved camming device (the Abalakov Cam) that resembles modern-day tricams. The traditional V-Thread is made by boring two holes with an ice screw; these holes connect in the back on a horizontal plane. An accessory cord is threaded through the holes and is tied off using a double fishermans knot, allowing climbers to rappel or use as anchors. While the traditional V-Thread is a required ice climbing skill, cleaner and stronger methods are available.

A-Threads: Vince Anderson tested ice threads in a vertical orientation and showed that due to the alignment of pulling forces was actually stronger this way. The A-Thread was born.

Zero Threads: As more focus is being placed on Leave No Trace principles, traditional threads have evolved to an environmentally friendly solution for rappelling. The Zero Thread, which can be placed either vertically or horizontally, is made using only the climbing rope. Not only is the Zero Thread stronger and faster, but it leaves behind no trash. Our first choice for rappelling is the vertically oriented Zero Thread.

Review:
V-Thread: Horizontally oriented and threaded with cord.
A-Thread: Vertically oriented and threaded with cord.   Stronger than the V-Thread.
Zero Thread: Vertically or horizontally oriented using the climbing rope. Stronger, cleaner, and faster.

CLIMBING IS DANGEROUS! SEEK QUALIFIED INSTRUCTION BEFORE UTILIZING TECHNIQUES OUTLINED IN THIS ARTICLE

CREATING A ZERO THREAD

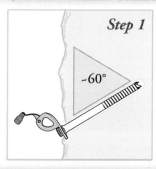
Step 1
~60°

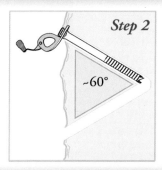
Step 2
~60°

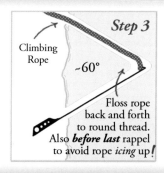
Step 3
Climbing Rope
~60°
Floss rope back and forth to round thread. Also *before last* rappel to avoid rope *icing* up!

ADDITIONAL PRO TIPS

• Quality of ice is essential, locate good solid ice

• Clean off any loose surface ice

• Bore holes at ~60° (see diagram)

• Use long screws (20-22cm)

• Second hole starts here

• Use screw to measure the distance to the second hole

• Holes at ~60° provide the greatest surface area and strongest threads

• Practice makes perfect threads

• Before starting the second screw it helps to line up the angle looking through the first hole

• Stop when the screw appears

• Avoid going past the first hole, it makes threading the rope harder

• After both holes are drilled, blow in the top to clear out any ice

• Bonus when feeding the rope into the top hole, it often makes the turn without needing a threading tool or wire

• Backup zero thread with a screw and draw, last down removes

• Proper backup tests the thread with no weight on the draw

• Properly dressed flat overhand knot

• At least 12" of tail

IF YOU WERE A CLIMBER

by Charlie Sassara

Regardless if you were a climber, a wanna-be, or straight up gumby, the 1978 Sports Illustrated cover photo of Jeff Lowe soloing Bridalveil Falls in Telluride blew your mind. The image and the idea behind it were humbling, motivating, shocking, and inspiring. In this moment we all wanted to be Jeff, but knew instantly that the bar was clearly above our heads. About the same time in Alaska, ice climbing was developing in the shadows of Keystone Canyon just north of Valdez. Early development was fostered by Andy Embick, with the likes of Carl Tobin, John Wieland, Roman Dial, Chuck Comstock, Bill Lorch, Bob Pudwell, Brian Teale, and yes, even Jeff Lowe setting the standards for sending bold vertical pillars with sparse (if any) protection. Contrast that to Anchorage where we borrowed gear, looked for partners, and waited for the newly blasted road cuts along the Seward HWY to freeze. While eager, we Anchorage types were clearly not "In the Game." We put up a few big routes, explored obvious lines at Eklutna Glacier, Knik Gorge, and

Harry Hunt climbing on Boulder Creek Pillar Left during an early ascent (Courtesy James Brady)

Portage but mostly scratched our way up modest frozen lines in hopes of tuning up for Valdez. That all changed when a brash East Coast kid with a hockey background named Steve Garvey showed up to consume every possible moss/ice filled seep within a mile of any highway from Anchorage to Homer to Valdez. His appetite was as insatiable as his imagination was expansive. When Steve, along with Jim Sweeney, completed Sans Ami in Keystone Canyon in 1987 the climbing elite took notice. Climbing onsite with no pre-placed gear, the route (now rated M8) was considered to be one of the hardest mixed routes in the world. Locally Garvey turned our attention to steeper mixed routes on Ptarmigan and woke us up to hard mixed lines and ethereal smears, moss drips and pillars we never even considered. Garvey climbed like a man possessed, a revolutionary, yet rarely ventured beyond hard–really hard–cragging. His love for family kept him close

Charlie Sassara climbing on peak 11,300 in the Alaska Range with David Stevenson (Courtesy David Stevenson)

to home. Sadly, Steve died in 1999 when his rope was cut through on a razor-like edge in Middle Canyon. Luckily not all accidents have bad endings. In November of 1985 Ernie Borjon, Dan McCabe, and I were testing each other for a possible winter ascent of Huntington with a climb of Dream of Brown Moose, a modest WI4 in Portage Valley. The ascent was unremarkable, but after a wind slab a thousand feet above us spontaneously released, the descent quickly became terrifying. As the curtain of snow shut out the world around us, chaos ensued. Dan and I were standing unclipped on the belay ledge. I grabbed the rope, while Dan tried to hide under a small overhang. The violence rolled on and on . . . then stopped. I had slid down twenty feet and was left standing directly atop Ernie's thighs. Dan had been ripped from his stance and disappeared. Ernie and I found Dan some 150' below. He was struggling to breath, his chest was flailed and face bloodied. Ernie went for help and I worked to keep Dan awake. Dan would recover. Huntington would wait. Fast forward a decade to the opening of the original Alaska

Navigating the glacier to access the climbs at Knik Gorge (Courtesy James Brady)

Rock Gym. In order to stay in business we quickly realized we would need to do our part to develop/cultivate a climbing culture. APU's Outdoor Program led by Dave McGivern joined the effort and a new generation of gym-spawned climber-punks were born. Today Anchorage climbers are stronger, more athletic, and better prepared than previous generations. This new foundation seems to be working, because it sure looks like they're having fun chasing down the dream that Jeff Lowe originally inspired.

Steve Garvey at Portage Glacier in the late 1980's (Courtesy Larry Nelson)

PARKS & DENALI HWYS 204

Cantwell

MATANUSKA RIVER VALLEY 132

VALDEZ 176

Talkeetna

EKLUTNA 76

Palmer

Wasilla

KNIK RIVER VALLEY 94

Eagle River

EAGLE RIVER 66

Anchorage

Valdez

ANCHORAGE & TURNAGAIN ARM 20

WHITTIER 56

Seward

SEWARD 162

Homer

HOMER 212

NABESNA 196

Nabesna

(Image Google Earth, Landsat / Copernicus)

Travis Mcalpine climbing Glass Onion
with Dane Ketner on belay

Harry Hunt on the first pitch of
Even Hookers Get the Blues
(Courtesy James Brady)

ANCHORAGE & TURNAGAIN ARM

Anchorage is a diverse city of over 350,000 individuals, the majority of which will never rope up to climb the many ice and rock lines that encompass it. Surrounded by the Chugach Range on one side and Turnagain and Knik Arm on the other, it is an adventurer's paradise right out the front door. That doesn't mean that it's always the best kind of adventures. You'll have to contend with semi-trucks and speeding cars on icy roads to get on the ice, but it's a perfect base camp for getting out to see Alaska. Rent a car, get a room, and spend every day exploring while returning to a warm place to sleep is what Anchorage is good for. There are also plenty of great restaurants. It is somehow a melting pot that had the top three most diverse public schools in the country, and with diversity comes delicious food.

Tara Moskiewicz climbing Scales on the Seward Highway, Turnagain Arm

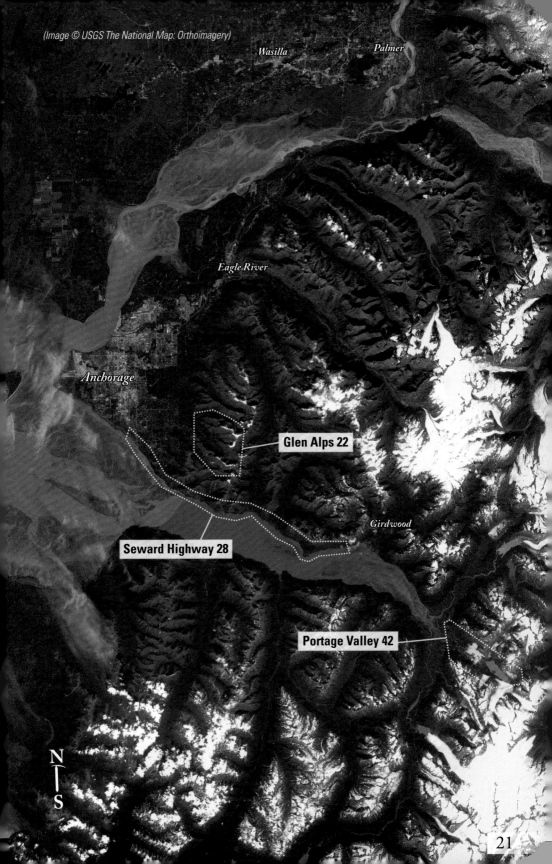

(Image © USGS The National Map: Orthoimagery)

Wasilla

Palmer

Eagle River

Anchorage

Glen Alps 22

Girdwood

Seward Highway 28

Portage Valley 42

N
S

(Courtesy Brady Deal)

Glen Alps

Distance: 3.5 - 7 miles

Approach: 1 - 3 hours

Difficulty: WI2 - WI5/6

ALERT: These routes are located in mountainous terrain with plenty of avalanche potential. Check conditions prior to approaching.

Access: The trailhead for these climbs can be reached from Glen Alps Parking Area. To get to the parking lot drive the Seward Highway to O'Malley Road, which is to the south from Anchorage. Drive about 4 miles east until just before the road makes a large left turn. Turn right onto Hillside Drive. Take a left on Upper Huffman; this is usually where you'll know quickly if your car is going to make the drive. The road is quite steep and has one of the sharpest turns in Anchorage. It is best not to even attempt this drive in icy conditions unless you have studs, 4 wheel drive, or chains. Upper Huffman comes to a stop sign and splits, take a right on Toilsome Hill Drive. Follow this road as it goes higher up the mountain and eventually turns into Glen Alps Road. The Glen Alps parking area will be on the left.

Description: Located in the Front Range behind Anchorage, these climbs are just a few in this giant state park. Even if you don't make it to the ice you'll probably have a great day just spending your time exploring. Williwaw can be translated to "tornadous winds" and you may find those here. Plenty of snow blankets these mountains and avalanches are a hazard. Snowmachines are allowed in some areas although ice climbers don't generally use them here. Skis or fatbike are the preferred mode of transportation, especially for Ptarmigan Peak as Powerline Pass is usually a quick trail used by many.

Quarter of a Climb

O'Malley Falls

Ptarmigan Pillar

Blue Funk

Even Hookers Get the Blues

P

Glen Alps Parking

Image © 2019 DigitalGlobe / Imap (Landsat / Copernicus)

23

O'MALLEY PEAK

Distance: 4.5 miles

Approach: 1.5 - 3 hours

Difficulty: WI2 - WI3

ALERT: Avalanches can and will happen in this area. Know your surroundings and be aware of current conditions.

Access: The first climb in this small area is located 3.5 miles from Glen Alps Trailhead. From Anchorage, drive to Glen Alps Trailhead, the same parking lot for Flattop. From the trailhead, hike toward Powerline Pass instead of going up Flattop Trail. Shortly after starting Powerline Pass Trail it will begin to head downhill. Take your first left on to a smaller trail. This trail will head you up to Little O'Malley through a steep snow gully. Once at the peak of the gully, you'll be in what is known as the Ballfield. Don't head up the peak following the ridge — stay in the valley and head directly toward the lake hidden at the end of the Ballfield. When you are near the lake, take a left and go down another steep decline to Black Lake. This is where you can find *Blue Funk*. From Black Lake, continue downward into the valley below and Williwaw Lakes. Keep right in the valley and you will run into *O'Malley Falls*.

Description: The trail to Little O'Malley is often well trafficked and the Ballfield is generally easy to follow. These climbs are located on the backside of O'Malley Peak and require persistence to get to but can be enjoyable, especially when done during an overnight trip to Williwaw Lakes. Be prepared for potential bad weather in this area, as winds have been measured in the valley as high as 145 mph.

The observant eye will notice a thin streak of ice to the left of Blue Funk in the image below. This is a climb called Black Lake and is normally done in mixed conditions, which is one of the reasons it is not highlighted in this current edition. In great conditions, it tends to be WI5 with some possible rock gear for protection. During other times it's a mixed adventure. It has been climbed to the peak above in a long day adventure.

(Courtesy David "Wildcard" Leon)

1. Blue Funk   WI2

12m

As a single objective, this may not be the most desirable climb. It is a small drip on the side of the cliff above Black Lake after dropping down from the Ballfield toward Williwaw Lakes. It is still a decent approach and will require most of the day for the trip out and back. Look for steps of blue ice above the lake on the right side of the cliff. | **Approach:** 3.5 miles from the trailhead. Located above Black Lake after dropping down from the Ballfield on O'Malley's northeast flank. | **Descent:** Vegetation tends to be minimal to non-existent at this elevation so bring V-threads for rappel. A walk-off may also be possible depending on snow cover and conditions.

2. O'Malley Falls   WI3

140m

While this climb has a fairly sizable approach (a few hours) it is reliable in forming each year. That doesn't mean that hazards do not exist - you have to cross avalanche terrain in the approach and then climb in possible avalanche terrain. Needless to say, it is important to pay attention to avalanche potential before climbing. The route consists of long, moderate climbing that has a few short curtains of WI3. | **Approach:** The climb is located on the backside of O'Malley when viewed from Anchorage, making it a longer trek than may be expected. | **Descent:** Vegetation tends to be minimal to non-existent at this elevation so be prepared to set a V-thread.

(Courtesy Michael Meyers)

PTARMIGAN PEAK

Distance: 4.3 miles

Approach: 1.5 hours

Difficulty: WI2 - WI5/6

ALERT: Avalanches can and will happen in this area. Know your surroundings and be aware of current conditions.

Access: From Anchorage, drive to Glen Alps Trailhead (the same parking lot for Flattop.) From the trailhead, hike, ski, or bike toward Powerline Pass. Follow Powerline Pass Trail approximately 3.5 miles to the north base of Ptarmigan Peak.

Description: Powerline Pass is a well trafficked trail and can vary from deep powder to packed snow and ice depending on the conditions. The climbs are located on the northern side of Ptarmigan Peak. *Even Hookers Gets the Blues* is typically an early season climb that fails to regenerate or gets buried in snow in the latter part of winter.

1. Even Hookers Get the Blues WI5/6

100m
Carl Tobin & Roman Dial

This route is located a ways up the snow gully known as North Couloir (some call it S-Couloir due to its large curved S shape) that splits the peak. The route climbs low-angle moderate ice for about half of its distance. Then the ice becomes steep and technical through to the finish. Above this climb is a steep slope that often spills snow down the face; be aware of conditions and be ready for spindrift. There is a piton anchor near the base of the first pitch that can be used or there is usually enough ice for a V-thread. An anchor exists at the base of the second pitch that may require some easy moves of mixed climbing to get to. Look for a big boulder on a flat ledge that often has webbing under it. The top of the second pitch also has an anchor that consists of one bolt

(Courtesy Nathaniel Bannish)

(Courtesy Joe Stock)

(Courtesy Nathaniel Bannish)

and a piton. | **Approach:** From Powerline Pass trailhead turn right once you are in-line with the N-Couloir. Head up the couloir until at the base of the route. | **Descent:** There are several anchors on the route that can be used to descend. The piton and bolt anchor on top of the second pitch should get you to the ledge where you can use the slings on the boulder to rappel back to the ground if using double ropes. Be prepared for a V-thread if additional rappels are needed.

2. Ptarmigan Pillar   WI2

72m

Located on the large rock rib between the N-Couloir and the basin that holds *Quarter of a Climb*. During the early season, this may form into a clean runnel of ice with a fast approach, and depending on how early it forms, the trail could be bike-able. After it snows, the climb often gets buried and may not be visible or climbable. The first pitch consists of a short 10m section and then moves to a second 60m tall pitch.
| **Approach:** Approximately 4.8 miles from the trailhead down Powerline Pass Trail. Continue past the large N-Couilor and to a rock rib that sticks out. The pillar is located on the right and should be easily visible in the early season. During the later part of the year it may just look like a snow gully. | **Descent:** Rappel the route using V-threads.

3. Quarter of a Climb   WI2

12m

This climb is short and wide. It's not really worth the long trip just for this short climb; but if you happen to be in the area or already climbed *Ptarmigan Pillar* and have some time left, then it could provide a few hours of fun climbing the variations. | **Approach:** Located on the backside of the peak when approaching from Glen Alps. About a mile past the gully for *Even Hookers Get the Blues,* there is a large basin on the right. This climb is located on a small rock step in this basin. Hike up the slope to the thin band with this climb. | **Descent:** There is no vegetation for anchors so bring screws or set a V-thread for the anchor on top of the ice. You can also belay from the rocks above. Walkoff the climb to the right.

Seward Highway

21

Distance: 0 - 0.2 miles

Approach: 0 - 10 minutes

Difficulty: WI2 - WI4/5

ALERT: Rock and ice falling between Anchorage and Girdwood is common especially after the 7.1 magnitude earthquake that occurred in the region on November 30, 2018.

Access: Getting to the Seward Highway climbs is as easy as driving the only road out of Anchorage that heads south. Follow the Seward Highway to your route of choice. Most routes should have mile markers listed under the approach information; this is the best locater to find the route. Remember, mile markers count down from Anchorage.

Description: The Seward Highway is an area that either causes one to fall into a moment of nostalgia or nausea depending on the person. With slick roads, fast moving cars, loose rock, falling ice, and just about every type of weather in a single winter season, this area can be one of those strange adventures that occurs within throwing distance of the car. There are not many areas in the country where the majority of the climbs can be done by anchoring to the bumper (nor recommended) so it tends to be a perfect after-work area. Most routes are immediately adjacent to the highway so be mindful of crossing the highway, belaying alongside the highway, and climbing above traffic that is often traveling at 60+ mph. For the safety of your vehicle, it is recommended that you park at the nearest pullout versus along the highway. It can be really tempting to park under the climbs, such as the vehicle in the picture above, but with all of the hazards involved it is better to park in the pullouts and away from the ice.

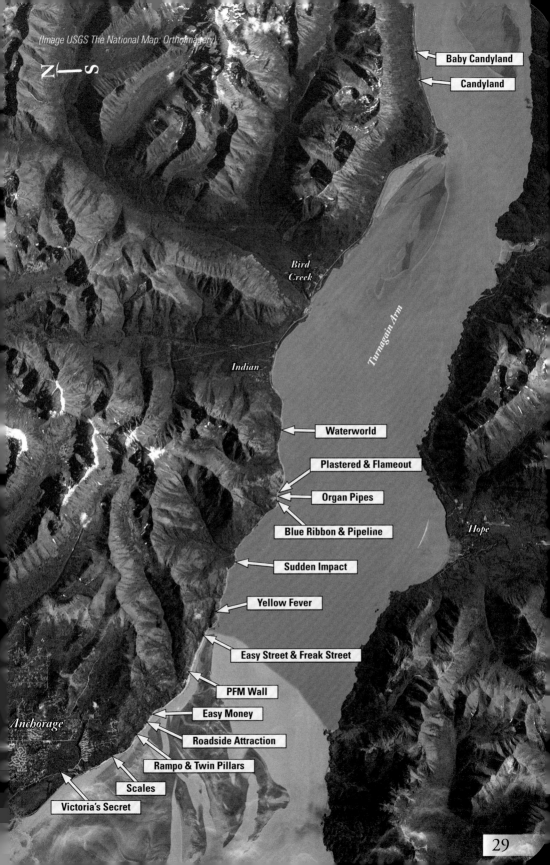

(Image USGS The National Map: Orthoimagery)

N — S

Baby Candyland

Candyland

Bird Creek

Turnagain Arm

Indian

Waterworld

Plastered & Flameout

Organ Pipes

Blue Ribbon & Pipeline

Hope

Sudden Impact

Yellow Fever

Easy Street & Freak Street

PFM Wall

Easy Money

Anchorage

Roadside Attraction

Rampo & Twin Pillars

Scales

Victoria's Secret

29

Ryan Campbell getting ready to head up Victoria's Secret. (Courtesy Sherrie Soltis)

1. Victoria's Secret   WI3

15m

This route is the only one located on this section of the highway. It is not on the main Seward Highway but off of the Old Seward Highway on the far side of Potter Marsh. It offers several options for ice and mixed climbing. There are some years where this climb may be non-existent and difficult to find. | **Approach:** From Anchorage, drive the Seward Highway south to Potter Valley Road, which is the first left after Potter's Marsh. After turning left onto Potter Valley Road, take another immediate left on Old Seward Highway. Drive approximately ¼ mile or until you see the route on the right. From the roadway you may have to negotiate hiking around or through water. | **Descent:** Alders exist for the rappel.

2. Scales Left and Scales   WI2

10-20m

Scales Left and *Scales* are well known nighttime climbs. Often the street lights along the Seward Highway will remain on, thus allowing adequate illumination for those wishing to hone their skills at 3AM. While you can climb to these lights be aware that they may also shut off without notice. Bring a head lamp just in case. *Scales Left* is the shorter (approximately 10 meters) of the two climbs, but at times steeper than its southern neighbor. *Scales* is the longer climb (approximately 15-20 meters) of the pair. | **Approach:** Mile 114.5. Located just after the weight station when heading south toward Seward. There is a parking area after the climbs on the left, although many people pull off the road below the climbs, which can be dangerous. The parking area is recommended. | **Descent:** Alders are scarce in the area so be prepared to place a V-thread if a sturdy anchor isn't available. *Scales* has a 2-bolt chain anchor that usually takes a step on to the moss to reach.

3. Rampo   WI2

22m

This route consists of a long ramp that comes down to a short curtain. It will often not form as well as *Twin Pillars*, especially at the start. Climb a short curtain and follow the ramp to the trees. | **Approach:** Mile 113.7. These climbs are located directly on the road and there is not a good pullout nearby. It is best to park further down the road (south) or pull off the road as far as possible. | **Descent:** At the top of the gully is a large tree that is often slung with webbing. There are also thin alders that can be used. V-threads can be difficult to place unless built low on the route.

4. Twin Pillars   WI2/3

20m

Twin Pillars Left is the easier of the two climbs and begins with a short and steep vertical curtain that can also be made easier if one climbs from the far left. The top of the climb past the bolted anchor is usually thin and the ice may end before the tree. Continue on dirt and some easy moss climbing to get to the top. *Twin Pillars*

This picture shows the Scales in thin late season conditions, while Scales is still climbable, Scales Left has all but disappeared

Right is often more vertical than its immediate neighbor but will usually include enough ice to be protectable. | **Approach:** Mile 113.7. These climbs are located directly on the road and there is not a good pullout nearby. It is best to park further down the road or pull off the road as far as possible. | **Descent:** At the top of the gully is a large tree that is often slung. There is a new 2-bolt anchor on the rock face above the first steep ice before the climb traverses right, it is the best to use and still gives you all the fun climbing.

5. Roadside Attraction   WI4

40m
John Bauman & D. Dobrowsky, 1979

The amount of ice on this wall can vary quickly, but when the ice is in it's not uncommon to see multiple parties. Steep ice for the first 10m makes up the crux then the ice leans back into a more moderate grade before topping out in alders. This wall can also provide mixed climbing for those wanting to challenge their skills.
Beware of knocking ice onto passing vehicles.
| **Approach:** Mile 113.3. Park directly across the street from the climb in a large pullout. Cars tend to drive fast in this area, so beware. | **Descent:**

Roadside Attraction is right on the road and several people have nearly been killed by falling ice while driving by. Be very careful about sending rock or ice down while climbing and park on the opposite side of the street.

There is a 2-bolt anchor on the wall that can be seen from across the street. The ice does not always reach the anchor so be prepared to create a V-thread or use vegetation.

6. Hypercard   WI4

40m
Carl Tobin & Friends

Located to the right of *Roadside Attraction* is a stellar route with a slightly higher difficultly rating than its neighbor. Depending on conditions, this climb can come in fat or very thin. Either way, expect more sustained climbing and possibly mixed conditions. | **Approach:** Mile 113.3. Park directly across the street from the climb in a large pullout. Cars tend to drive fast in this area, so beware. | **Descent:** Alders exist at the top of these climbs; however, be prepared to place a V-thread if a solid anchor isn't available. There is a 2-bolt anchor on the top that may or may not reach the ice and can be seen from the parking lot.

Marc Davis on his first ice climb, an unlisted flow in the parking lot of McHugh Creek during a beautiful winters day

7. The Beast   WI4/5

40m

Located to the right of *Hypercard*, this pillar offers a steep and often dicey route for those looking to push their climbing skills to the next level. Depending on conditions, protection may be difficult to find and even less so towards the top. Bring your short screws just in case. (Note: The smear to the right of *The Beast* is called *The Howling* and the smear to the left is called *Fright Night*. Both routes require high skill and possibly rock protection.) | **Approach:** Mile 113.3. Park directly across the street from the climb in a large pullout. Cars tend to drive fast in this area so beware. | **Descent:** A fixed anchor is located on the bench at the top.

8. Easy Money   WI3

20m

Graham McDonald & Ernie Borjon, 1981

Climb a relatively short, but somewhat vertical pillar approximately 10 meters to a ledge. From the ledge, another short section of ice separates you from the top. Like many climbs along Turnagain Arm, this route can get a good amount of late-day sun and is often detached from the rock during warm spells. | **Approach:** Mile 113. Park just past the climb in a pullout and hike

back toward Anchorage. The route is located just off the road. | **Descent:** A 2-bolt anchor exists on the top of the route for rappel.

9. PFM   WI4/5

31m
Ernie Borjon & Graham McDonald, 1981

PFM Wall (often called Weeping Wall) offers numerous ice and drytool routes for those looking to push their limits. Rock and ice protection is good to have on hand; these routes are not recommended for beginners.

PFM is defined as a large hanging cicle that often requires some drytooling to access. Climb through several bolts (some may be covered in ice) to reach the thicker ice above. Above the cicle, some fat and less difficult ice prevails. Beware of bad rock. This wall has undergone many changes over the years with large portions of it falling down. This climb and the surrounding ones have remained relatively consistent, but to the right and left is unstable. The leftward sloping rail of ice that meets with *PFM* near the top is called *Cold Snap WI4* (FA: Bob Crawford & Martin Martinez, 1989) | **Approach:** Mile 111.5. Park in the large pullout and hike over the small hill to the climb. | **Descent:** Alders exist at the top of some of the climbs but it is also recommended to bring V-thread material.

10. Easy Street   WI3

20m
Bob O'Brian & Doug VanEtten, 1984

A large flow that can form as two separate climbs or into one wide connected piece. It receives plenty of sunlight and can separate quickly from the wall during a warm spell. It has been known to completely erode and then appear again later in the season due to the high volume of water flow. | **Approach:** Mile 110.7. Park in a pullout further down the road or pull as far off the road as possible. There is not much room for a vehicle off the side of the road near the climb. | **Descent:** Alders exist on top for rappel.

11. Freak Street   WI2+

15m
Dan McCabe & Steve Davis, 1984

There are plenty of variations to this climb on the surrounding ice, but *Freak Street* follows the main weakness up a short, moderate flow on the left that comes out at a small corner. (Image located on the next page) | **Approach:** Mile 110.6. This climb is right on the highway. Hike from the parking area along the road. | **Descent:** Alders exist at the top for anchor and rappel.

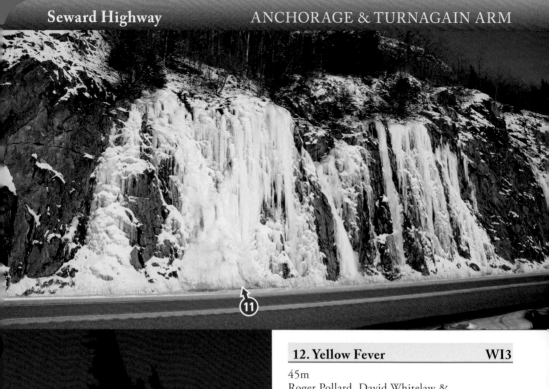

12. Yellow Fever   WI3

45m

Roger Pollard, David Whitelaw &
Jay Rowe, 1988

Higher up the cliff than many of the other climbs
along the highway, it got its name from the color
of the ice that forms. This climb can be a fun ice
line in the thick years or an interesting mixed line
during the thin ones. Pitons or rock gear may
be helpful on this one. | **Approach:** Mile 109.9.
Park on the water side of the road in a small
pullout and hike back down the road until under
the climb, which is located 150m up the hillside.
Head up through the trees staying slightly right
to avoid the rock bands on the left. | **Descent:**
Rappel the route. V-thread material may be
necessary.

13. Sudden Impact   WI3

25m

This climb takes dangerous highway belays
to a new level. Located right on the corner of
the road, you'll have to keep your head up for
oncoming traffic to belay. Climb about 10m of
nearly vertical ice to a more gentle finish and
alders. | **Approach:** Mile 108.6. Located just
across the street from the parking area. Dodge
traffic on the corner to reach the base of the
climb. | **Descent:** There are plenty of alders but a
new 2-bolt anchor is in place for an easy rappel.

14. Blue Ribbon   WI3

50m

Depending on the size of the flow, it can include some easy mixed climbing in sections. *Blue Ribbon* is the major left flow while *Pipeline* is the major right flow. During some years, the ice may connect in the middle to form one large sheet. It is also common for much of the climb to be under a layer of thin snow, making it difficult to see just how much ice there is. | **Approach:** Mile 106.5. This long highway climb is located at the pullout for Windy Corner. Park on the opposite side of the road and hike to the base of the climb. | **Descent:** It is possible to rappel the route with two ropes; however, you can also hike right about 50 meters and rappel on alders with a single rope down the gully that holds *Organ Pipes*.

Blue Ribbon and Pipeline in thin conditions during a particularly warm spring day. These climbs may form thick enough to connect during a good year but are also often thin at the start. They are often overlooked as they are right on the road and usually covered in a layer of snow, but they can be an enjoyable long climbs with no approach. The Department of Transportation occasionally has plans to blow up certain parts of this area, while they may not have put those plans into action yet, its only a matter of time.

15. Pipeline   WI3

50m

This is the right-hand line of ice that descends from the tree ledge above. *Blue Ribbon* is the left-hand line. It is often thin in the middle, but usually ends with a thick portion of ice before the top-out. There are plenty of trees above the lip that can be used for an anchor. There are also some thin alders in the middle of the climb that may be used for a center anchor, although most climbers will continue to the top. | **Approach:** Mile 106.4. This long highway climb is located at the pullout for Windy Corner. Park just across the road in a wide parking lot and hike across the road to the base of the route. | **Descent:** It is possible to rappel the route with two ropes; however, you can also hike right about 30 meters and rappel on alders with a single rope.

16. Organ Pipes   WI3

25m

This climb gets its name from the row of ice that resembles organ pipes. There is usually an area of thin ice through various steps to reach the short crux that ends on a ledge of trees. | **Approach:** Mile 106.4. Park just across the road in a somewhat wide parking lot and hike across the road to a debris gully. These climbs are located about 30m up the hillside in a broken looking section of rock with several flows of ice. | **Descent:** Rappel the route using trees on the left edge of the climb. This will put you higher on the hill and can be done using a single rope.

17. Plastered   WI3

25m

This climb is located in a small alcove and faces to the right. It is probably the most popular line at the Windy Corner area and there is usually at least one party on it during a cold weekend. The ice can be thinner than you would expect so make sure to bring short screws. *Right Variation (WI3):* The climb splits near the top; going to the right is slightly harder. After topping out the ice, you will need to traverse left under the rock to find the anchor. Descent and approach information is the same. | **Approach:** Mile 106.4. It is best to park across the street and hike to the base of the climb. | **Descent:** There is a 2-bolt anchor on top of each variation that should be used to rappel. Bolts save our alders and trees by reducing the wear to the vegetation.

18. Flame Out   WI4

17m

Steep and sometimes thin, this shorty will give you a good run for your money. There are nearby bolts that are for a newer mixed climb. | **Approach:** Mile 106.4. Hike a moderately steep section of snow to the base of the route. | **Descent:** A 2-bolt anchor exists on top. You may still need to bring some webbing in case there are no rappel rings.

19. Waterworld   WI2/3

12m

This little alcove and nearby walls on the highway sport numerous options for those climbers looking for short, easy to moderate routes. If you're looking to hone your ice skills, this is a great place to ice boulder or learn how to place ice pro. Depending on where the ice falls, one may find a bit of mixed climbing too. | **Approach:** Mile 104.8. Park, then climb. | **Descent:** There are plenty of large trees and alders on top of these routes, although some require long slings to make the ropes run smoothly. A long walk-off is also possible to the left of the area but requires some route-finding.

20. Candyland   WI3/4

100m
Steve Davis & Dave Miller

If good conditions exist, a few top-to-bottom flows can be found in the center of the wall. Most climbing parties tackle the climb in 3-pitches with the first and second tiers being the longer and more difficult sections. Don't be surprised to find some mixed conditions at the top of the first tier. Approximately 150 feet left of the large flows is a 45 foot high mass of baby blue ice. If toproping is your preference, this is a great place to set a rope and can be accessed by foot. | **Approach:** Mile 94.8. Park on the water side of the road (mile 95.3) in a pullout, and cross to the other side. Hike along the road until you are in line with the climb. You have to cross the railroad tracks and it is illegal to do without a permit. Permits can be picked up at the Alaska Railroad Police Department in downtown Anchorage (320 W 1st Ave, Anchorage). Please pick up a permit to limit access issues to any area that crosses the railroad tracks. | **Descent:** Above the third tier alders are available for belay and rappel. If planning to rappel the route, be prepared to place V-threads. Otherwise, gain access to the trail above then hike the trail towards Anchorage until you find a safe descent route down to the highway. Some down climbing on ice may be required on the descent.

21. Baby Candyland   WI3

90m

These climbs offer some of the best plastic ice in the area and seem to form more often than their larger neighbor to the north. All tiers are relatively short and moderate in difficulty. Large ledges with often dense alder brush separate the tiers. This area is highly recommended for those new to the sport or those who are learning to lead. | **Approach:** Mile 94. Park on the opposite side of the road and cross the street toward the cliff. Hike toward the climbs but do not hike down the railroad tracks. You have to cross the railroad tracks and it is illegal to do without a permit. Permits can be picked up at the Alaska Railroad Police Department in downtown Anchorage (320 W 1st Ave, Anchorage). | **Descent:** Dense alders are available for belay and rappel on a few routes. If alders are not available use ice screws for anchors. The climbs are relatively short and rappelling the route is recommended as a safe walk-off may be difficult to find or require a long hike. Be prepared to place V-threads when descending on routes without alders.

Portage Valley

Distance: 0.2 - 1.4 miles

Approach: 10 minutes - 1 hour

Difficulty: WI2 - WI6

ALERT: Avalanches are common in this area, with multiple near-fatalities through the years from climbers attempting the ice lines. Be very aware of conditions before proceeding.

Access: Portage Valley has easy access from Anchorage. Please note that mile markers count backward from Anchorage (mile 127) to Seward (mile 1). Drive south on the Seward Highway toward Seward for 48 miles (from downtown Anchorage to mile marker 79). Turn left after the Alaska Wildlife Conservation Center and before a large wide right bend. The exit comes quickly so slow down ahead of time as it can be dangerous in the winter. Parking for *Indecision* is at mile 80.3 in a large parking area on the left hand side of the road. The rest of the climbs are located down Portage Glacier Highway.

Description: Portage Valley is probably the most fickle area in this book. Attempting to climb at the right time of the season is vital for many of these climbs and even then they could disappear in a matter of days. Rain can fall at any time of the year loading the upper slopes with new snow and washing away the climbs. Routes like *Dreams of Brown Moose* are a gamble anytime after the beginning of the season when avalanches tend to flood the gully. One such climber was buried beneath the climb and only managed to survive after being dug out by his climbing partner. *Hands Across the Water* requires traversing the lake by kayak, or foot if the lake is frozen. During the later parts of the year, the lake turns into a massive playground with any number of people getting out of Anchorage for a quick trip across to the glacier. You may be able to just make out the small dots in the picture above, showing just how vast the valley is. Portage Glacier is located just around the bend in the center of the photo but it is melting quickly. In 1914, the glacier covered what is now the Begich, Boggs Visitor Center. As early as a few years ago, the glacier was still easily visible.

(Image © DigitalGlobe / Image Municipality of Anchorage)

Hands Across the Water

Portage Lake

P

Tallman

Gutterboy

Follies

Bullwinkle

Dreams of Brown Moose

Rainbow Bridge

Death Lizard

Skin Game
The Fringe

P

Secret Lover

Luckyman

Gingus

Five Fingers Area

P

Indecision & Fate is the Hunter

43

PORTAGE FLATS

Distance: 1.3 miles

Approach: 30 minutes

Difficulty: WI3 - WI4

ALERT: Avalanches can and will happen in this area. Know your surroundings and be aware of current conditions. Crossing the railroad tracks is illegal without a permit. You can get a permit at the railroad office in downtown Anchorage.

Access: Drive the Seward Highway south from Girdwood to the large pullout (mile 80.3) on the east side of the highway a ½-mile north of the Portage Highway intersection.

Description: This area is geographically first when entering Portage Valley but is probably one of the longer approaches. It requires a hike across the flats to ice that is just barely visible from the road. Depending on conditions, this can be a quick approach or a long trek through the snow. It also requires you to cross the railroad tracks, which necessitates a permit from the Alaska Railroad. This can be obtained free from the Alaska Railroad Police Department in downtown Anchorage (320 W 1st Ave.) There are only a few climbs in this area but they're still worth the hike when in good condition.

1. Indecision   WI4

250m
Peter Sennhauser & Charlie Head, 1980

Visible from Portage Glacier Highway and Seward Highway, this must-do route offers a day of WI2-4 ice with great views. Start at a wide apron of ice that may or may not be accessible due to the rarely frozen pond at the base. If open water prevents access to the base, then climb *Fate is the Hunter* (route immediately right of *Indecision*) to the top of the first step then bushwhack left until you get back to *Indecision*.

Indecision just after a warm spell. Due to the large volume of flow, this waterfall often has a dark hole at the base where the ice doesn't freeze. This can make the climb more interesting as well as dangerous. It is best to climb after a good freeze cycle.

| **Approach:** From the pullout you have a few options. First option is to follow the railroad tracks south then east into Portage Valley for about 30-45 minutes before turning left and making a b-line to the ice. Please note that hiking within the railroad right-of-way without approval to do so is a fine-able offense. The second option is hiking / skiing / snowmachining directly from the roadside pullout to the route. This, however, can be difficult due to the abundance of wetlands in the area. | **Descent:** Rappelling the route via vegetation or V-thread is common. One can also hike off down to the right of the route. Don't be surprised to find many of the adjacent trees with an abundance of webbing.

2. Fate is the Hunter WI3

37m
Ernie Borjon & Ned Lewis

Located to the right of *Indecision*, this short piece of ice follows a wide and semi-steep apron up a moderately sloped ramp to the trees above. When the lower section of *Indecision* is blocked by open water, parties will often climb this route to the trees above then bushwhack to *Indecision*. This is a good route for toproping. | **Approach:** Same as *Indecision*. | **Descent:** Rappel from vegetation or V-thread.

FIVE FINGERS

Distance: 0.2 miles

Approach: 10 minutes

Difficulty: WI2 - WI3

Access: From Anchorage, drive the Seward Highway south for approximately 1 hour then turn left on the Portage Glacier Highway as if going to Whittier (mile 79). Note that at the time this book was being written, the Seward Highway between Girdwood and Ingram Creek was under construction. Once complete, the intersection of Seward Highway and Portage Glacier Highway will be in a slightly different location. From the intersection, drive approximately 3.2 miles to the pullout (may or may not be cleared of snow) just past a bridge over a small creek. Park in the pullout, then hike along the base of the ridgeline for approx. 5-10 minutes and the climbs will be up and to your right. **Description:** An excellent destination with a handful of routes for beginners and moderately skilled ice climbers. Climb or toprope one route then hike through the trees a short distance and repeat. It's not uncommon for various parties to leave their toprope for others. Due to the moderate angles of these routes, snowfall can make finding good ice a frustrating task.

3. The Pinkie WI2

20m

Located to the far left, the short section of WI2-3 ice is ideal for toproping and those new to the sport. | **Approach:** Drive the Seward Highway south from Girdwood then turn east towards Whittier at the Portage Glacier Highway. Drive approximately 3 miles to the pullout on the right, just after a small bridge. If the pullout is full or not cleared of snow, you'll need to find a spot alongside the highway. During times of low snowfall it is possible to drive beyond the pullout and park in a clearing at the base of a large avalanche chute. Find the creek that runs along the base of the ridge, follow it until the climbs are directly above, then hike up to the base of the ice. Moving between the routes is common and there is typically a well trampled path between all. | **Descent:** Rappelling from vegetation is the quickest and most common, but a walk-off exists to the far right.

4. Ring Finger	**WI2**

52m

The second climb from the left is a bit longer and wider than *Pinkie* and also provides plenty of WI2-3 climbing. May require multiple pitches. | **Approach:** Same as *The Pinkie*. | **Descent:** Rappelling from vegetation is the quickest and most common, but a walk-off exists to the far right.

5. Middle Finger	**WI2**

52m

A decent pitch of WI2-3 with some short and steeper sections on the right-hand side. | **Approach:** Same as *The Pinkie*. | **Descent:** Rappelling from vegetation is the quickest and most common, but a walk-off exists to the far right.

6. First Finger   WI3

55m

Probably the most climbed ice in the area, this route can be expansive enough to allow a party on either side. The left side is more WI2-3 whereas on the right there is a 15-20 ft. pillar option about 2/3 of the way up. Parties of the right hand side can belay from a treed area that is mostly out of the way from icefall and provides shelter on snowy days. | **Approach:** Drive the Seward Highway south from Girdwood then turn east towards Whittier at the Portage Glacier Highway. Drive approximately 3 miles to the pullout on the right just after a small bridge. If the pullout is full or not cleared of snow, you'll need to find a spot alongside the highway. During times of low snowfall it is possible to drive beyond the pullout and park in a clearing at the base of a large avalanche chute. Find the creek that runs along the base of the ridge, follow it until the climbs are directly above, then hike up to the base of the ice. Moving between the routes is common and there is typically a well trampled path between all. | **Descent:** Rappelling from vegetation is the quickest and most common, but a walk-off exists to the far right.

7. Little Boy   WI2

25m

This route holds the 5-meter steep, free hanging pillar at the top. During good flow years this route may merge with the one to the right. | **Approach:** Same as for *First Finger*. | **Descent:** Rappel from trees or alders.

8. The Thumb   WI3

52m

Located farthest to the right, this ice can be thin when the other fingers are in thick. During times of early freezing there may be short vertical sections towards the top, which can become less steep as the season progresses. | **Approach:** The same as *First Finger*. | **Descent:** Rappelling from vegetation is the quickest and most common, but a walk-off exists to the far right.

MIDDLE GLACIER CANYON

Distance: 0.5 miles

Approach: 15 minutes

Difficulty: WI2 - WI6

ALERT: Avalanches can and will happen in this area. Know your surroundings and be aware of current conditions.

Access: From Anchorage, drive the Seward Highway south for approximately 1 hour, then turn left on the Portage Glacier Highway as if going to Whittier. Note that at the time this book was being written the Seward Highway between Girdwood and Ingram Creek was under construction. Once complete the intersection of Seward Highway and Portage Glacier Highway will be in a slightly different location. From the intersection drive approximately 4.2 miles to the Williwaw Salmon Viewing pullout. Hike to the Trail of Blue Ice. You should see a wooden bridge

ahead that crosses a small stream and heads directly toward the mountain. Follow this over the creek and traverse the cliff left. Follow the base of the cliff until it ends and you round into Middle Glacier Canyon. You can also head directly toward the canyon but often takes more of a bushwhack. **Description:** As with the rest of Portage this is a no go zone during avalanche conditions. A good destination when avalanche potential is low and routes are in FAT. A heavy concentration of high quality climbs and the area testpiece *Gingus* all reside inside the canyon.

9. Death Lizard   WI2

62m

Located just to the left of *Rainbow Bridge*. This is where many of the avalanches above drain out creating a wide fan. A mellow climb that follows between two rock ridges and ends above *Rainbow Bridge*. | **Approach:** From below the climb ascend a small ridge until directly below *Rainbow Bridge*. The climb starts to the left. | **Descent:** Small alders exist on the top of the climb but a V-thread may be necessary.

10. Rainbow Bridge   WI3

60m

This climb is a single pitch of moderate ice located on the left side of the canyon when approaching. The length of the climb can depend on the amount of snow covering the top. Usually climbed in a single 60m pitch of ice that spreads wide on this small rock outcropping. | **Approach:** From the base of the valley ascend a small hill by hiking up the left side. This will put you directly at the base of the climb. | **Descent:** Alders exist on top of the climb but may require travel over snow covered ice. V-threads can be placed at the top of the ice.

11. Secret Lover   WI2

77m

The next flow of ice to the right of *Luckyman*. A somewhat gentle flow that can also be surprisingly enjoyable. It is often used as a rappel pitch for *Luckyman*. Follow the thin flow into the trees

above. | **Approach:** From the valley floor, a short scramble may be necessary to reach the ice. | **Descent:** Plenty of vegetation for rappel.

12. Luckyman   WI4

100m
Charlie Sassara & Robert Frank, 1982

A classic must-do in Portage Valley. *Luckyman* is a two-pitch climb that can be climbed in several ways. The most straight-forward is to climb moderate ice up to a narrow dihedral with rock on the left and ice on the right. Once in the dihedral, you can find alders midway up the climb that make for excellent protection or belay stations. From there it's a pitch of WI4 to the top. | **Approach:** Located on the right side of the canyon. Starts up a small ice-filled gully before moving right to the climb. | **Descent:** Alders on top with possible V-thread in the middle for the second rappel. This climb can be difficult to rappel due to the thin nature of the ice in the middle of the climb. An easier rappel exists by hiking right to the top of *Secret Lover*; this shorter climb has plenty of vegetation for the rappel. There are bolts that exist on and near *Luckyman* but they are for a rock route and are often buried in winter.

13. Skin Game   WI4

74m

First climbed after *The Fringe*, these two climbs are further up valley than the rest on a small wall known as the Fringe Wall. They cover a bowl of rock that is often visible through the thin ice. They tend to be dark as they form thin, but protectable, across the face. Bring short screws. *Skin Game* follows the left flow with several variations on the start. | **Approach:** Continue up valley following the left side of the river until across from the climbs. There are a few short uphill sections to get to the base of these climbs. They do not come into view well until halfway up the valley. | **Descent:** Alders exist at the top and it is recommended that you bring long ropes due to thin ice. Hike right 30m to a gully and rappel the gully.

14. The Fringe   WI3/4

68m
Charlie Sassara & Dave McGivern, 1985

The right flow on the Fringe Wall. Follow a thin smear of often veer-glassed slabs into a corner. It is recommended that you belay at the top of the dihedral and then finish the final 15m pitch

to the alders. A long rope may make it all the way to the top. | **Approach:** Continue up valley following the left side of the river until across from the climbs. There are a few short uphill sections to get to the base of these climbs. They do not come into view well until halfway up the valley. | **Descent:** Alders exist at the top and it is recommended that you bring long ropes due to thin ice. Hike right 30m to a gully and rappel the gully.

15. Gingus	WI6

80m
Steve Garvey & Paul Wharton

A classic testpiece of the area. The climb ascends a left facing dihedral and much of it is hidden from view until nearly under the climb. The top can be seen from halfway up the gully and looks like an intimidating smear at the top of the canyon. A committing lead that may require rock gear even in good conditions. | **Approach:** Continue up canyon following the right side of the river. You'll have to hike uphill for a short time following the base of the cliff. Keep an eye out for the base of the climb on the right. | **Descent:** Alders exist at the top for rappel. Bring V-thread material as a backup.

This image shows just the top half of Gingus, there is more climbing below. An excellent route that requires all types of protection and is a worthy notch for any hardman ice climber to add to their belt.

VISITOR CENTER AREA

Distance: 0.15 - 1.4 miles

Approach: 15 minutes - 1 hour

Difficulty: WI2+ - WI4

ALERT: Avalanches can and will happen in this area. Know your surroundings and be aware of current conditions.

Access: Located 55 miles from Anchorage is the Begich, Boggs Visitor Center for Portage Glacier. These climbs are located on both sides of the valley, as well as across the lake. This is the most spread out area in Portage Valley. All of the climbs can be accessed by parking at or nearby the visitor center.

Description: There are some excellent lines located in this area with high potential for all types of natural hazards. *Hands Across the Water* requires travel over Portage Lake, which occasionally decides not to freeze all season. Other climbs, such as *Dreams of Brown Moose* and *Bullwinkle,* sit in one of the more dangerous avalanche zones in the area, with the climbs on the north side of Portage River tending to be the more easily accessible. They still require some obnoxious side-hilling or a hop across the river. Overall it's a great area with *Follies, Hands Across the Water,* and *Dreams of Brown Moose* equaling a golden triangle of quality climbing.

16. Follies   WI4

75m
Jim Hale, Gary Bocarde, & Doug Billman, 1975

This excellent route is usually done in two pitches as there is a good belay in the middle of the climb. From the middle belay, climb through steep ice that ends in a moderate finish to the top. | **Approach:** Getting to *Follies* may be the crux of the day as it can take a long time if you're forced to go from the road and follow the cliff edge. Option 1: Park on the road close to the bridge and hike down to the river's edge on

the mountain side. With heavy snow, this is a cumbersome path and could take as long as an hour to reach the climb. Option 2: Portage River tends to be shallow in this area and sometimes it is a lot easier to cross the river and then head direct to the climb, rather than to try side-hilling. | **Descent:** There are trees on top of the climb to use for anchors and descent. There is also a walk-off possible to the left of the climb. Hike down the snow slope to the left of the climb and then traverse back to the base.

17. Gutterboy   WI2+

30m

This is a pitch of gently rolling ice that is located just above the river. There are other climbs nearby that apparently didn't form when the original lines were climbed but now come in as good, solid ice lines. | **Approach:** The most ideal path to this climb would be to cross Portage River and head straight to the climb. The river occasionally freezes but usually ends up being open with ice patches. Check the depth and if it is shallow then head across. If the river is impassable, then you

can side-hill along the cliff edge to the base of the route. This is usually a time-consuming and less enjoyable path. | **Descent:** Alder bushes and trees exist on the route to set up natural protection for rappel stations.

18. Tallman   WI3

92m

Bob Dugan & David McGivern

On the hillside, there is a climb that forms a 10m pillar that does not usually connect. This small pillar forms the crux section of *Tallman*. During a heavy snow year, the majority of the climb may be under snow but when exposed *Tallman* creates a long thin line of ice. | **Approach:** Traverse the cliff edge by crossing the bridge and turning left before the tunnel. This traverse can be tricky with sections of open water below and up and down traversing. Once at the base of the climb, hike / climb the steep snow slope to the base of the climb. | **Descent:** Alder bushes and trees exist on the route to set up natural protection for rappel stations.

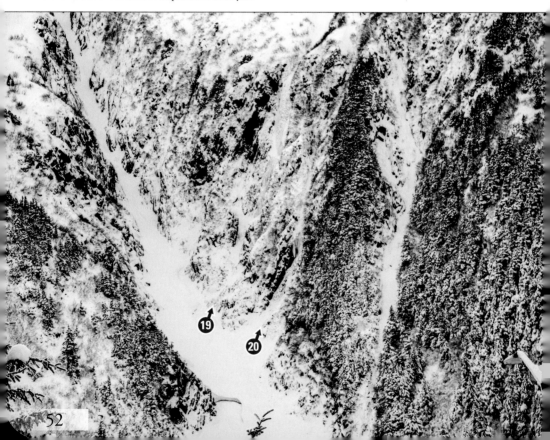

19. Dreams of Brown Moose   WI4

130m
Jim Hale & Gary Bocarde, 1975

ALERT: *Dreams of Brown Moose* is within a large avalanche chute. Know your surroundings and be aware of the snow conditions before venturing onto this route!

This is one of the most popular routes in Portage Valley despite the objective hazard – it is at the base of a large avalanche chute. It is highly recommended to stay clear of this route when avalanche conditions exist. Begin the route with a windy WI2-3 section followed by a shorter yet steeper section of ice. The last pitch is an enjoyable WI4 that narrows as it goes up. You'll know you're at the top when you see the rappel anchor in the rock on your right. | **Approach:** Located high in an avalanche-prone gully to the south of the Visitor Center, the approach doesn't develop much of a trail. Park east of the Visitor Center and pick a path; leading directly to the climb bushwhacking your path, the entire hike is about 1 mile. Ascending the avalanche gully is usually the crux and most dangerous portion of the approach. | **Descent:** Rappel the route. A bolted rappel anchor exists at the top, then use V-threads.

20. Bullwinkle   WI3

77m

ALERT: *Bullwinkle* is within a large avalanche chute. Know your surroundings and be aware of the snow conditions before venturing onto this route!

Easy WI2 climbing leads up to a curtain that poses the crux of the climb. From the curtain, more moderate ice leads to the top. Depending on the conditions of the curtain, the difficulty of the climb may vary. | **Approach:** Same approach as *Dreams of Brown Moose.* | **Descent:** Vegetation exists at the top of the climb; however, due to the length of the climb, be prepared to set a V-thread.

Portage Lake can be a wonderful place to explore during a cold snap but the lake is also dangerous and unpredictable. Be wary of the ice depth and never approach the face of the glacier, where calving can occur even in the winter.

21. Hands Across the Water   WI4

230m
Charlie Sassara & David McGivern, 1983

This excellent climb has multiple variations and possibilities depending on how the water falls over this face. Visible from the Visitor Center this big flow cascades from high on the mountain and is a great day adventure. | **Approach:** When the lake is frozen, the approach is a cruiser hike directly across to the climbs. When the lake is not frozen, it requires a watercraft to reach the base. | **Descent:** V-threads necessary.

54

Marcin Ksok on Dreams of Brown Moose in the Visitor Center Area, Portage

WHITTIER

Let's be honest, Whittier is not exactly a desirable destination for many. A small town that shutters much of its doors during the wintertime and weather that would give Juneau a run for its money. There's a reason the moniker, "nothing shittier than Whittier" exists. This could be part of the reason that the town is easily forgotten in the winter, but during the early season there could be a wealth of traffic free ice. Weather in the area is fickle and tends to be in one day and gone the next. And to make matters worse, pretty much all of the hills around Whittier are prone to avalanches so be familiar with conditions. On the flip side, when conditions are good you will be rewarded with plenty of challenges. The prize line would be if the pillar on *Horsetail Falls* ever connected to the ground, it would make a steep and committing line.

The only real feasible way to reach Whittier from Anchorage is to drive through the Anton Anderson Memorial Tunnel. The tunnel is 3 miles long and is an amazing feat of WWII engineering. Drive 55 miles from Anchorage and turn left on Portage Glacier Road at mile 78.9 of the Seward Highway. Continue on Portage Glacier Road until you reach the tunnel entrance. At this point you will have to pay a round-trip toll, which at the printing of this book is $13 for vehicles under 28ft long. If you're driving a motorhome then it will cost you more. Drive through the tunnel and the first climb will be just to your left. Continue on the main road a few more miles and you'll be in Whittier proper.

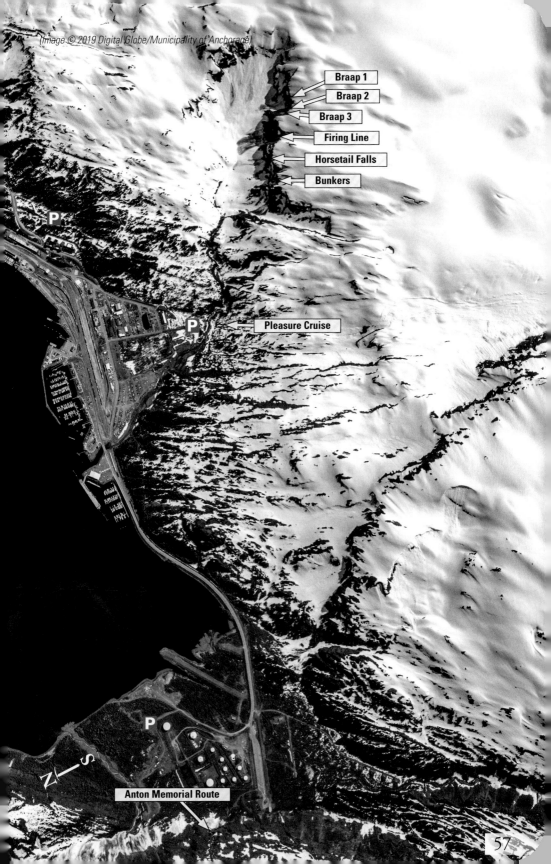

(Image © 2019 Digital Globe/Municipality of Anchorage)

Braap 1

Braap 2

Braap 3

Firing Line

Horsetail Falls

Bunkers

Pleasure Cruise

Anton Memorial Route

57

HORSETAIL FALLS

Distance: 1 mile

Approach: 30 minutes

Difficulty: WI4 - WI4+

ALERT: Avalanches tend to make this area too dangerous after the early season. Be aware of conditions before climbing.

Access: Once you pass through the tunnel, continue on the road toward Whittier, you'll pass Whittier Creek just after the cruise ship dock. Turn right and cross over the tracks. Continue through town until you come to a 4-way stop. Drive straight uphill toward the Buckner Building (big and ugly). Take a right onto Shotgun Cove Road and drive 0.2 miles, then take a right onto Reservoir Road, which may not be marked. There is a gate at the bend in the road and a sign for Horsetail Falls Trail. Park at the gate and follow the main trail for 1 mile. If you cannot find the trail, follow the path of least resistance around the hill to the valley. Once in the valley, head directly for the base of the climbs.

Description: Horsetail Falls is a beautiful area in winter and summer. Access is generally easy, as there is a trail that leads directly to the valley; however, this trail may only be visible during low snow cover years. Whittier is an unpredictable area that is best only when conditions are just right — when snow levels are low and temps are cold. Even though it may not look like a dangerous area, the slopes above deposit large debris fields on the climbs and there are no climbs in this guide from Whittier that are safe from avalanches.

1. Braap 1   WI4+

145m
Jay Rowe & Peter Haeussler

This route and the next two were named after the sound that snowmachines make as they rip up the hillside. They can be very loud and numerous in this area when there is good snow cover. Located climber's left of *Braap 2*. Hike moderately steep snow and rock and possibly over avalanche debris. Climb moderate ice, snow and rock to the base of a wide curtain of ice. Climb the steep and wide curtain to a finish pitch of more steep ice and snow. | **Approach:** Located in the same drainage as the next two climbs. This is the climb on the left side of the gully. | **Descent:** Rappel the route. V-thread material is necessary.

2. Braap 2   WI4+

145m
Jay Rowe & Peter Haeussler

Climb a pitch of moderate snow and ice to another pitch of steeper snow and ice. Finish on a steep pitch of the same. | **Approach:** Located in the same drainage as *Braap 1 & 3*, this is the middle route. Hike moderately steep snow and possible avalanche debris to the base of the route. | **Descent:** Rappel the route. V-thread material is necessary.

3. Braap 3   WI4+

145m
Jay Rowe & Peter Haeussler

Depending on conditions, there may be two starts to the climb. The right start is a wide, long, and moderately steep pitch of ice. The left start is shorter and steeper and may require mixed skills at the top. Climb 1-2 more pitches of snow and ice to the top. | **Approach:** This climb is located in the same drainage as *Braap 1 & 2* and is climbers right in the gully. Hike moderately steep snow and rock to the base of the route. | **Descent:** Rappel the route. V-thread material is necessary.

4. Firing Line   WI4+

150m

Climb a pitch of moderate and possible thin ice to the landing above. Follow with another pitch of moderate and thin ice to the top. There is often a small, short section of ice just to the left of the start of the climb. | **Approach:** Hike a long and moderately steep section of snow to the base of the route. | **Descent:** Rappel the route. V-thread material is necessary.

5. Horsetail Falls   WI4

90m

This route is climber's left of *Bunkers* and climbs toward the obvious pillar. It is not known if this pillar has ever touched down, but if it had, it would likely be the most difficult climb in the valley. | **Approach:** From the valley floor, hike moderately steep ground to the base of the climb. | **Descent:** Rappel the route. V-thread material is necessary.

6. Bunkers   WI4

140m

The first climb to the right when hiking up the valley. From the landing, climb moderately steep ice to the top. There are several variations for the start with varying difficulties,; it can get thinner near the top-out. | **Approach:** From the valley floor, hike a steep section of snow to the base of the climb. | **Descent:** Rappel the route. V-thread material is necessary.

Sherrie Soltis on Horsetail Falls, the dagger looms above (Courtesy Michael Meyers)

Horsetail Falls   *Pleasure Cruise*

WHITTIER CREEK

Distance: 300 meters

Approach: 5 minutes

Difficulty: WI2

ALERT: Avalanches can and will happen in this area. Only good during an early season freeze before any heavy snowfall.
Access: Parking for this climb is behind Begich Tower at the back of town. Follow the main road into town; just after crossing Whittier Creek, take a right on Whittier St. After 0.3 miles take a right on to Glacier Ave. Drive another 0.3 miles until the road ends in a turnaround. Park here and hike directly ahead for the climb.
Description: A good place for beginning leaders and those who wish for a long mellow jaunt through the ice up to a beautiful viewpoint over Whittier. Most experienced climbers will find this easy enough to be tedious. There are some surrounding flows to be had at a greater difficulty, but for the most part you should go to Horsetail Falls if you're experienced and want adventure.

7. Pleasure Cruise	WI2

380m

Behind Begich Tower there are several large flows that lazily meander their way down the mountain to combine at Whittier Creek. These flows come in often during an early freeze and when the snow is minimal. This is ABSOLUTELY a no-go zone if the route appears covered in snow or there is even a hint of avalanche potential. During the late season, this may just look like a big snowfield. Most of the route is steep scrambling on thick ice in a sort of choose-your-own-adventure style of climbing. *Pleasure Cruise* follows the left flow at the split in the middle and goes to the top left of the rim. The top of the flow opens into a wide valley and has some incredible views. There are plenty of variations as well as other small climbs on both the right and left sides of the valley that can offer some enjoyable and mostly easy climbing. | **Approach:** From the parking area, hike over a small hill directly toward the river. It can be best to put your crampons on here. Then you can hike up the river until the climbing starts. | **Descent:** There are plenty of trees for several rappels and V-threads should fill in for the rest. There is a possible walk-off that is on the far left when looking toward the cliff. There is a small snow band that snakes its way down the cliff. The walk-off requires some down scrambling and is better when there is snow cover. There are also places for rappel from trees during the hike down.

TUNNEL AREA

Distance: 0.5 miles

Approach: 15 minutes

Difficulty: WI4

ALERT: Avalanches can and will happen in this area. Know your surroundings and be aware of current conditions.

Access: Located just to the right of the tunnel when driving toward Anchorage. This climb pours down from the mountain about 200m to the north. It is not legal to park near the tunnel or anywhere at the lineup for tunnel entry. The best way to approach this climb from the Whittier Tunnel is to drive toward Whittier and turn left at the Y in the road just after you cross the railroad tracks. Head toward Whittier Campground and take a left onto Tank Farm Road. This will head toward a shooting range. Further access via vehicle from this point may be hindered by the amount of snow and you may need to park and begin walking early depending on snow cover.

Description: The Tunnel Area currently consists of a single climb that forms early in the season and can have variable conditions. Whittier seems to have its own weather patterns and doesn't feel like following the rest of the state. It can be warm when Anchorage is cold and sometimes these climbs don't form at all. This climb gives you a great view over the town of Whittier and Passage Canal.

8. Anton Memorial Route   WI4

150m

This route is located just to the right of the Whittier Tunnel when looking at it from the Whittier side. It is the large obvious flow on the side of the mountain. When in good condition, this route can be around 200m and really nice with the lower half of the flow becoming thick

ice. On the upper half of the route, conditions change and there may be some thin sections with possible mixed climbing needed to connect the ice. In poor conditions it ups the adventure. Often a short window exists on this climb when condtions are right for good ice and low avalanche potential. Most parties will only climb the first 3-4 pitches where the ice is thick and there are plenty of placements. | **Approach:** Drive as far as you can toward the climb (follow Access information) and then hike toward the climb. There may be some alder bashing necessary but try and follow the roads as long as possible. | **Descent:** V-threads will be necessary.

The Anton Memorial Route in really good conditions.

Robert Suenram eyeing the second pitch of Anton Memorial Route during a perfect weather window

63

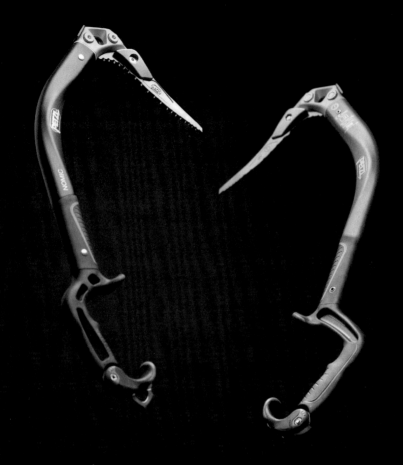

NOMIC & ERGONOMIC

Steep and steeper.

The new NOMIC maintains its world-famous swing and excels at climbing steep ice. Crafted for swinging and hooking into delicate or mixed lines, the ERGONOMIC is the choice for those climbing steeper or overhanging terrain. Both tools feature an overmolded dual handle, adjustable GRIPREST, modular head, and hydroformed shaft. www.petzl.com

Photo © www.kalice.fr

 Access the inaccessible®

Travis Mcalpine scratching his way up rock that is eventually covered by Spruch Pitch later in the season. Thin conditions just means additional challenges

EAGLE RIVER

Eagle River is a playground for outdoor adventure enthusiasts and with good reason. The valley is surrounded by steep, imposing peaks that hold serious mountaineering and skiing objectives. Mt. Yukla has become somewhat of a testing ground for budding Alaskan alpinists with a growing number of routes along its walls. Polar Bear Peak and Hurdy Gurdy also have multiple ice lines to be found. Leading from Eagle River Nature Center and over Crow Pass to Girdwood is Crow Pass Trail, a popular overnight hike that can make the nature trail seem crowded on a summer day. While many of the main routes are in the Echo Bend area, additional and worthy climbs lie beyond, tucked away in the numerous side valleys.

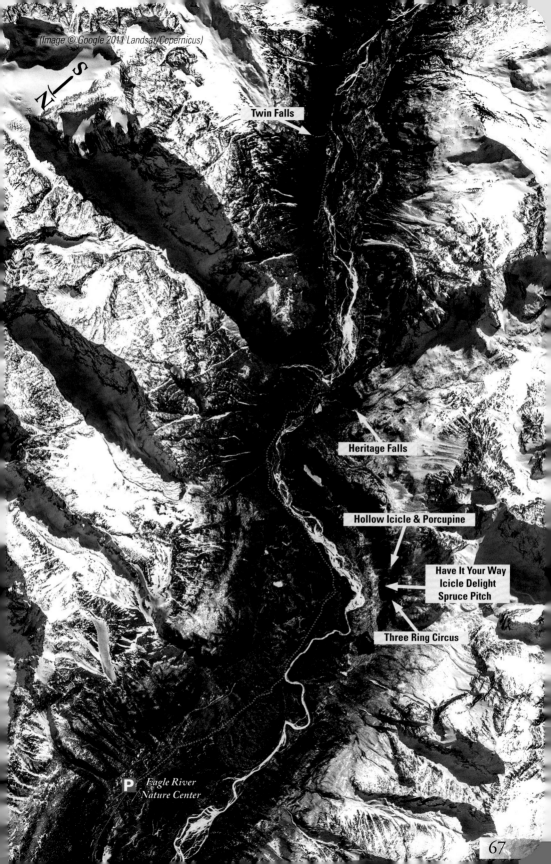

(Image © Google 2011 Landsat/Copernicus)

Twin Falls

Heritage Falls

Hollow Icicle & Porcupine

Have It Your Way
Icicle Delight
Spruce Pitch

Three Ring Circus

P Eagle River
Nature Center

67

Eagle River

Access: From Anchorage, drive the Glenn Highway north then take the Eagle River Loop exit and follow it east and then north as it goes across Eagle River, then back up the hill to a major stoplight at Eagle River Road. Take a right and follow Eagle River Road to the very end, approximately 11 miles from the intersection, and pull into the Eagle River Nature Center parking lot. Please note the parking lot is not large and can fill up quickly, so make sure you arrive early and do not park in the street.

ECHO BEND

Distance: 3.5 miles

Approach: 1 - 1.5 hours

Difficulty: WI2 - WI4+

ALERT: Avalanches can and will happen in this area. Know your surroundings and be aware of current conditions.

Access: Park at the Eagle River Nature Center (a daily fee for parking will be necessary) and walk to the back to the Nature Center. Follow the well-established trails for 3 miles to Echo Bend. Now that you are alongside the river, look straight south across the river and *Hollow Icicle* should be easy to see. Make your way across the river and either

find an established trail through the brush or just b-line straight to the route. Another option, and one that doesn't require parking at the visitor center, is snowmachine up the river from one of the open access points. Before doing so you will need to verify with the State Department of Natural Resources that snowmachine access is open on the river. This access is also valid for *Heritage Falls* and *Twin Falls*.

Description: Echo Bend may seem like a somewhat lengthy hike compared to the Seward Highway or even areas like Eklutna Canyon, but when you're surrounded by imposing peaks in a valley that seem to ooze adventure, you'll hardly notice the time. This is a great area to climb single pitch ice for the day or to explore long multipitch lines. The crux can be keeping your feet dry, as crossing Eagle River may require running through calf-to knee-deep waters.

1. Hollow Icicle   WI4+

100m
Conrad Guenther & Bruce Roberts, 1985

Choose a left start on a 12-15 meter near-vertical pillar or take the more moderate angled ice to the right. Above that is a short section of lower angle snow or ice. From here you can climb the rest in one pitch or you can climb another section of ice to the base of the pillar and then set belay for the final crux. The later option will put your belayer in harms way. Begin climbing the pillar, which is literally a tube of ice that gets thinner towards the top. Breathe easy at the top when you look down into the inside of the tube and see the teeth of your shorty screw protruding. | **Approach:** Follow Echo Bend approach. Once across Eagle River head straight for the climb. | **Descent:** Alders at the top of the route will provide anchor for rappel; however, the next rappel will require V-thread.

(Courtesy Richard Baranow)

2. Porcupine   WI3

31m
Steve Davis & Ned Lewis, 1989

This is a short but fun chimney that begins at the top of the first pitch of *Hollow Icicle*. It traverses a snow/ice ramp to the right of *Hollow Icicle* and tends to form thin. It may require rock gear as well as screws depending on conditions. This climb is hard to see from below but is a good second option if *Hollow Icicle* tells you no. | **Approach:** Climb the first pitch of *Hollow Icicle* and start this climb from there. | **Descent:** Alder bushes exist above the second pitch to rappel. A V-thread is necessary to get down safely off the first pitch. You can also traverse left to the top of *Hollow Icicle* and then do a double rope rappel.

3. Have it Your Way   WI2

45m
Conrad Guenther, George Fuller & Steve Davis, 1984

A popular climb that is about 50m to the left of *Spruce Pitch*. Follow thick ice on big bulges as it moves right to the trees above. There is a hidden 8m pillar about 30m above the climb for those looking to extend the adventure. | **Approach:** Head directly toward the climb from the river. | **Descent:** Plenty of trees on top for anchors and rappel.

Left: This climb doesn't see as much traffic as Spruce Pitch but can be enjoyable and challenging climbing where it is easy to set up a toprope. (Courtesy Sherrie Soltis)
Right: Sherrie Soltis high on a relatively anemic Spruce Pitch with Josh Pickle on belay. (Courtesy Michael Meyers)

5. Spruce Pitch   WI2

18m
Conrad Guenther & George Fuller, 1984

As the most consistent ice at Echo Bend, *Spruce Pitch* sees plenty of traffic. During the early season or in low-water years, there may be several separate flows in this area; during a good season it will connect into one large flow. Despite the early season thin possibilities, there is usually a few runnels available to connect to the top. There are opportunities to make this climb harder by going to the left or right of the main line. Depending on conditions, a few fun mixed climbs can be toproped from the same anchor. | **Approach:** Cross Eagle River; the best place to cross can change from week to week. There is a trail on the other side of the river that can be difficult to find, but game trails usually persist in the trees. When in doubt, head directly toward the climb. | **Descent:** There is a large tree at the top of the climb to use as an anchor and for rappel.

4. Icicle Delight   WI3

12m
Conrad Guenther, 1984

This short climb can pack a punch depending on conditions and which part of the pillar you decide to climb. It is located in a rock corner to the left of *Spruce Pitch* and may form into a steep pillar of WI4 on the left or a more mellow climb of bulges on the right. Expect plenty of hanging icicles. | **Approach:** Head to *Spruce Pitch* and this climb is in a rock corner on the left. | **Descent:** Trees exist on top for rappel.

(Courtesy Michael Meyers)

6. Three Ring Circus   WI3+

275m
Conrad Guenther & George Fuller, 1984

This is the longest route in the area when you add in the occasional snow sections. Depending on conditions and time of season, this route may barely even be visible under all of the snow or avalanche debris. It is important to know the snow conditions before attempting the climb. Ascend easier sections of snow and ice to the first pillar. Continue more moderate pitches of ice separated by snow. | **Approach:** Most of the approaches to these routes are relatively straightforward. Head toward the climb after crossing the river. You will probably need to ascend a decent amount of snow before accessing the first pitch. | **Descent:** Alders exist on the route, but V-thread material is recommended.

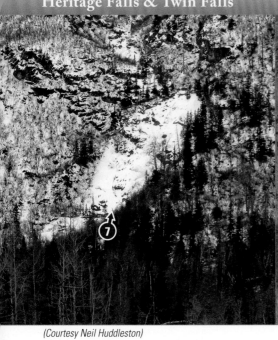

(Courtesy Neil Huddleston)   *(Courtesy Neil Huddleston)*

HERITAGE FALLS

Distance: 5.5 miles

Approach: 2.5 hours

Difficulty: WI2

7. Heritage Falls   WI2

110m

Heritage Falls, while being a decently long climb, is probably not going to see much traffic due to its distance from the trailhead. There are two climbs that come together here, so pick your route and head up moderately angled ice. | **Approach:** After hiking for 5 miles from the Eagle River Nature Center, staying on the main trail, you will be across from *Heritage Falls* on the opposite side of the river. Cross the river here and head up Heritage Creek another half mile to the climbs. It should be noted that snowmachine and fatbike access is typically restricted to no further than about mile 5. | **Descent:** It is possible to bush-whack down or rappel from trees.

TWIN FALLS

Distance: 7.5 miles

Approach: 3.5 hours

Difficulty: WI4

8. Twin Falls   WI4

100m
John Bauman & D. Dobrowsky, 1980

Seldom done because it is 7.5 miles from the Eagle River Nature Center. Some steep scrambling will get you to the base of the first pillar. After the first pitch, turn the corner and head into the second, more difficult pitch. There is a walk-off descent on the left (northeast) from the top. | **Approach:** After 7.5 miles on the trail from Eagle River Nature Center you'll finally come to *Twin Falls*. Turn left and head up a short 0.2 mile approach to the climb. | **Descent:** There is a walk off descent on the left (northeast) from the top. Alders exist for the rappel from the top pitch but a V-thread will likely be necessary to get back to the ground.

Jon Cobb climbing to the right of Miller Might at Eklutna Glacier with Freer's Tears and Road to Nowhere in the Background (Courtesy Sherrie Soltis)

The Mountaineering Club of Alaska (MCA) is a 501(c)(7) non-profit corporation, founded in 1958, whose core purpose is to strengthen Alaska's mountaineering community through camaraderie, education, adventure and volunteerism.

The MCA is based in Anchorage and offers training events, mentorship program, mountaineering trips, a historical library, monthly mountain related presentations and newsletters. MCA maintains 8 huts in the local Chugach and Talkeetna Mountains for public use, basic frame structures that offer safety and comfort in amazing locations. If you would like to become an MCA member to help maintain huts and sustain activities please visit us:

MOUNTAINEERING CLUB OF ALASKA

mtnclubak.org

Thanks for your support

EKLUTNA

The Eklutna River system begins at Eklutna Glacier, located approximately 25 miles due east of Anchorage within the Chugach mountains. Meltwater from the glacier creates the Eklutna River which then flows 4 miles north into the somewhat secluded, 7-mile long Eklutna Lake. This lake has long been a source for much of Anchorage's clean drinking water. Downstream of the lake the Eklutna River flows into a deep and windy canyon before passing under the Glenn Highway and emptying into Knik Arm. Recreational opportunities of all types abound along this entire drainage. However, ice climbing opportunities are only found near the glacier, referred to in this book as Eklutna Glacier, and in the canyon just upstream of the Glenn Highway, referred to as Eklutna Canyon.

(Courtesy Michael Meyers)

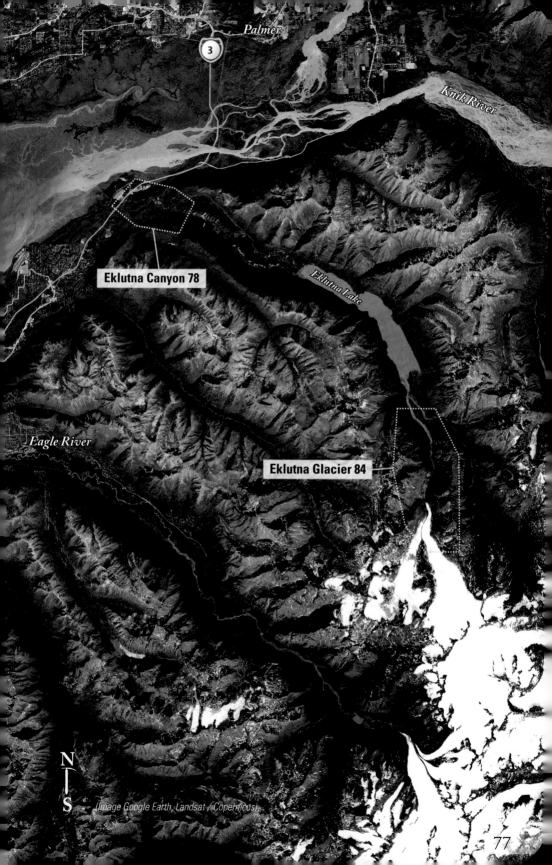

Palmer

Knik River

Eklutna Lake

Eklutna Canyon 78

Eagle River

Eklutna Glacier 84

N
S

(Image Google Earth, Landsat / Copernicus)

Eklutna Canyon

(Courtesy Michael Meyers)

6

Distance: 0.25 to 1.3 miles

Approach: 5 - 30 minutes

Difficulty: WI2 - WI4

Access: If coming from Anchorage, drive the Glenn Highway north approximately 23 miles to the Thunderbird Falls turnoff. Take the turnoff and follow the Old Glenn Highway for approximately 0.3 miles then take a right into the Department of Natural Resources (DNR) maintained Thunderbird Falls Trail parking lot. If coming from the north, you'll want to exit the Glenn Highway at the Eklutna Lake / Thunderbird Falls exit, then turn right on the Old Glenn Highway. Drive past Eklutna Lake Road, over the Eklutna River bridge and immediately turn left into the Thunderbird Falls Trail parking lot. The parking lot requires a current State Parks Pass sticker on the windshield of your car. However, if you don't have one you can purchase a day pass at the trail kiosk. From the parking lot you have a few approach options. The first is to access the creek immediately below the parking lot. A steep and often very slippery trail to the left of the latrines, followed by a short walk through trees and brush, will put you at the river. Follow the river up and keep your eyes out for the routes. Second approach option is to follow the Thunderbird Falls Trail for 0.5 miles and then descend into the canyon upriver. The trail will emerge where the canyon splits. Keep your eyes open, as there are a number of locations where one can easily descend to the river by foot without rappelling.

Description: Eklutna is comprised of two very good areas. Eklutna Canyon is probably the most popular climbing area outside of the Seward Highway and *Ripple*, before alaskaiceclimbing.com came along, was once considered the most climbed piece of ice in Alaska. An excellent day trip from Anchorage, it's unlikely you'll find yourself alone in the canyon during the weekend and you may need to continue down canyon to get away from the crowd. There are also many mixed lines that exist in this area.

(Image © 2019 Digital Globe)

Annie Greensprings

Boonesfarm

Ripple

TJ Swann

Cham Ripple

P

Mad Dog

N
S

79

(Courtesy Michael Meyers)

1. Mad Dog   WI3/4

25m

Harry Hunt, Dave Lucey & Ernie Borjon, Dec. 1995

Mad Dog is one of those climbs you walk by and say, "Oh, looks like it's not coming in this year". Then the next year you have a blast playing on fat ice. It usually forms thin and is difficult or impossible to protect and resembles a mixed climb more than water ice. When it's in you'll enjoy good protection and a relatively easy route. | **Approach:** The first good flow of ice that you come to on the river after only a quarter-mile of hiking. | **Descent:** The are large trees on top of the route for an anchor. Bring slings for the rappel.

2. Cham Ripple   WI2/3

25m

Greg Siewers & Scott Mignery, 1984

Another climb that doesn't always fully form. When well-formed, the crux will likely be the top of the climb, where it can be pulling over moss or a nice short curtain. If it is in thin conditions, it can be hard to protect, which ups the difficulty slightly. | **Approach:** Continue hiking the river until under the climb half a mile into the canyon. Currently the only climb listed in this area that is on the left side of the canyon, although plenty of mixed lines exist on the left side. | **Descent:** Many alder bushes are available for setting up anchors.

3. TJ Swann   WI3

30m
Doug Van Etten & Marty Schmidt, 1983

TJ Swann gets a lot of traffic as it is before *Ripple* and has been forming up really nicely the last few years. When it is picked out, the pillar section feels like a ladder, but it's still an enjoyable climb with several possibilities to make it more difficult. The small roof left of the middle adds an additional challenge for the willing. There is a climb that forms about 30m left of *TJ Swann* that requires a scramble to get to and seems to just pour through the woods. It doesn't always form but can be an enjoyable second line to set up when you are in the area. (WI2). | **Approach:** Several hundred meters past *Cham Ripple*; this climb is easily identifiable by the steep face and left side that partially covers a roof. It is located just off the river and will require a short scramble on snow to reach the base. | **Descent:** Plenty of trees on top for anchors and rappel.

(Courtesy Michael Meyers)

4. Ripple   WI3

65m
Paul Denkewalter & Gary Bocarde

Ripple is a classic of the area and always forms
a nice large wide flow. If you are going to have
multiple parties on this route at the same time,
then it is best to stop above the first curtain.
Ripple flows right down to the river. The route
can be done in a single rope stretcher pitch but
it is best to bring a 70m. The first anchor is just
above the first curtain on the right side. There
will also usually be slings around trees on both
sides of the flow. Climb through a section that is
longer than it looks and then find the anchor on
the top of the climb. The bolts have been recently
replaced. | **Approach:** Approximately 1.2 miles
from the car. Located right on the river and is the
largest flow in the canyon. | **Descent:** Bolts are
located on the right immediately above the first
curtain. On the left hand side above the curtain is
a tree that may be hard to reach if using a single
rope to rappel. Bolts located on a right-facing
rock face exist at the top of the climb. Bring a
V-thread in case you miss the anchors. Tie knots
in the end of the rope!

5. Boonesfarm   WI3

60m
Paul Denkewalter & Gary Bocarde

Most of the climbing on *Boonesfarm* is moderate
WI2 that leads up to a set of bolts right before
the crux. After the crux pillar there are more
bolts at the top. | **Approach:** 1.3 miles up the
canyon, this climb is on the right hand side. The
beginning is a moderate slope of WI2. | **Descent:**
A 2-bolt anchor exists on top for rappel and
another 2-bolt anchor is above the first crux.

6. Annie Greensprings   WI3

20m

This climb is the last before what used to be the
dam. It is best in the late season and forms an
often chandeliered curtain at the start, which
is the crux. From the curtain, lead up an easy
section to the finish. There are a lot of mixed
climbs in this canyon and the opposite side of
this route also holds some good climbing.
| **Approach:** Just past *Boonesfarm* on the right
hand side. Approximately 1.4 miles up the
canyon from the parking area.
| **Descent:** Trees on top for anchor and rappel.

(Courtesy Michael Meyers)

(Courtesy Michael Meyers)

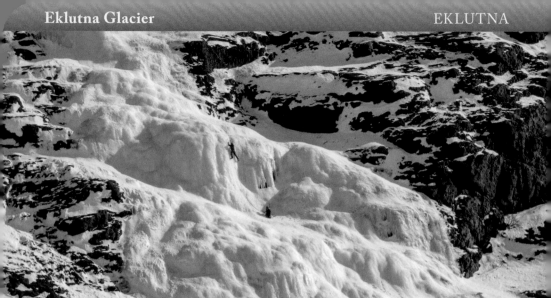

Climbers on Miller Mite (Courtesy Matthew Tucker)

Eklutna Glacier

Distance: 12 - 15 miles

Approach: 45 minutes - 2 hours

Difficulty: WI2 - WI6

ALERT: This is an alpine adventure area where avalanches are common and the hazards are numerous.

Access: From Anchorage, take the Glenn Highway north toward Palmer. Take a right for the turnoff to Eklutna at mile 26.5 and then another right at Eklutna Village Road. Another immediate right will put you on the Old Glenn Highway. After .4 miles take a left onto Eklutna Lake Road. Drive 9 miles until a gate at the end. Depending on snow levels the parking lot may not be at the same location as that used by summer recreationists. Eklutna Lake Road follows the left side of the lake but is only accessible by recreational vehicle. The trail is open to off-road vehicles Sunday - Wednesday and closed to ATV's December 1st - March 31st. When there is adequate snowpack, the area is opened daily to snowmachine access. One thing to keep in mind: ATVs and snowmachines are not allowed past mile 12.9 of the Eklutna Lake Trail. Beyond that, one must either ski, bike, snowshoe or hike. When Eklutna Lake freezes, the distance from the parking lot to the routes is shortened by about 1-2 miles. Approach information for routes start from the Serenity Falls Public Use Cabin located 12 miles from the trailhead.

Description: Eklutna Glacier is one of the more striking areas in this book. The approach is along a beautiful lake that provides Anchorage with much of its drinking water and surrounded by 7000-foot peaks that provide their own amount of challenge. At the back end of the valley, these climbs seem to guard the entrance to the glacier, which is receding quickly from the majestic mountains above. There are many classic lines and testpieces in this area that will provide a challenge to any who enter it. There are also great places to go as a beginner climber and moderate lines for the intermediate climber. It is important to always pay attention to conditions, as avalanches are common from the steep snow slopes above.

Hats Off to Herman

Freer's Tears

Mitre Mite

The Nose

Road to Nowhere

Lucey in the Sky & Headstone Pillars

Eklutna Man

Miller Mite

Dirty Harry

Iron Curtain

Serenity Falls

Serenity Falls Cabin

S
N

Image © Google 2016 Landsat / Copernicus

1. Serenity Falls   WI4

200m
Charlie Sassara, Mike Miller, Brian Canard &
Karl Swanson, 1987

Clearly visible from the Serenity Falls Cabin, this
is the second major piece of ice on the right, just
after crossing the Eklutna Glacier drainage. Rack
up at the base for multiple pillars of blue ice,
separated by snow slopes. During the later parts
of the season this climb will probably become
less appealing than its neighbor as snow begins to
fill up parts of the line. | **Approach:** A relatively
straightforward approach. From the Serenity Falls
hut, walk shortly back to the bridge that crosses
the river. Cross the river and follow the main trail
for 0.5 miles until under the route. From the
trail, hike through trees to the base of the climb.
| **Descent:** Look for anchors on nearby alders or
bring gear for a V-thread.

2. Iron Curtain   WI4

200m
Nick Parker & Helmut Schriddiger, 1979

Iron Curtain is the larger flow to the left of
Serenity Falls. Usually a more aesthetically pleasing
climb as the pitches of *Serenity Falls* fill up with
snow. Generally broken up into three pitches. The
first is a short 15m climb up WI2 to a snowfield,
continue up the snowfield to the base of another
pitch of ice. After around 60m, you'll pop out on
to another snowfield, follow this to the curtain,
which may form up to 50m. | **Approach:** The
same approach as *Serenity Falls* but is located
another 100 meters down the trail. These climbs
may have a sizable amount of avalanche debris to
navigate to the base. | **Descent:** Look for anchors
on nearby alders or bring gear for a V-thread.

(Courtesy Michael Meyers)

The picture above shows the Dirty Harry Area in late season conditions with much of the ice having melted. This area can fill entirely with ice during a long cold snap.

3. Dirty Harry   WI2/3

60m

This area is referred to as the Dirty Harry Area and has many lines on a wide sheet of ice that has been reported as being able to form 300m wide, though it normally creates partially independent lines. Most of the routes are moderate WI2 climbing, but there are several areas that form into slightly steeper WI3. A great place to spend a day or to take newer climbers. Several lines are established with the area first being explored by Mike Miller, Dave Whitelaw, and Amy Johnson. | **Approach:** 1.5 miles from the Serenity Falls hut. Follow the trail across the bridge. Stay low on the river around the bend and look for this large flow of ice on the right-hand side before the river constriction. | **Descent:** Alders exist in some areas but V-threads are also recommended.

4. Miller Might   WI4

200m
Bob Crawford & Martin Martinez, 1988

The first large flow on the left side of the canyon when approaching from the hut. It may not look like much at times, but is generally a large wide flow of enjoyable ice. A great route with plenty of variation opportunity. The header image for this area on page 84 shows a few climbers on route. During the first ascent in 1988, they had to either skirt the glacier or travel over it to reach this climb. | **Approach:** 1.8 miles from the Serenity Falls hut. A short hike from the hut will put you across the bridge, then head up canyon for 1.8 miles following low by the river. Leave the river before it constricts and head left following the slope; this can be a slog in deep snow. During the right conditions, you may be able to follow the river through the gap and head left once at the base of the climb. | **Descent:** V-threads for the rappel.

5. Eklutna Man   WI5

200m
Bob Crawford & Carl Swanson

A testy climb that changes yearly due to environmental conditions; usually done in 4-5 pitches but doesn't see a lot of successful ascents. The best start is down left on a low-angle slab of ice that leads to a right-angling snow/ice gully. Move right after the ice and follow the ledge as the ice thickens to the base of the main sheet. This may require some mixed climbing and rock protection. Climb the first crux to moderate WI3 terrain until under the roof. Most parties will descend here, although it has been continued through the upper roof...but conditions need to be perfect. The upper section was climbed by Eddie Phay and Harry Hunt at WI6. | **Approach:** From Serenity Falls hut head up canyon for 1.8 miles following the river. Leave the river before it constricts and head left up the slope; this can be a slog in deep snow. During the right conditions you may be able to follow the river through the gap and head left once at the base of the climbs. These are between *Miller Might* and *Mitre Might*. | **Descent:** Rappel the route using V-threads and possible rock gear.

(Courtesy Sam Volk)

6. Lucey in the Sky   WI6

200m
Dave Lucey & Kristian Sieling, Mar. 2001

A rarely completely formed flow that is between
Eklutna Man and *Headstone Pillar*. It is a series
of tempting, disconnected pillars that form thin
when in. Start direct on technical slabs into the
main flow. During the first ascent, Dave Lucey
took a 30-foot fall leaving his tool high on route.
He finished the pitch with his belayer's tool.
| **Approach:** From Serenity Falls hut head up the
valley for 1.8, miles following the river. Leave
the river before it constricts and head left up the
slope; this can be a slog in deep snow. During the
right conditions, you may be able to follow the
river through the gap and head left once at the
base of the climbs. Access the climbs by ascending
a short piece of easy ice into a small bowl below
Eklutna Man. Follow the snow slope right to the
base of the climb. | **Descent:** V-threads for the
rappel.

7. Headstone Pillars   WI5

180m
Harry Hunt & Dave Miller

Considered by many who climb it to be one
of the best in an area that includes multiple
classic lines. A series of steep pillars in the upper
headwall form the crux of the route. Climb
moderate thick ice to the base of the headwall and
follow the pillars up through the roof system. |
Approach: From Serenity Falls hut head up the
valley for 1.8, miles following the river. Leave
the river before it constricts and head left up the
slope; this can be a slog in deep snow. During the
right conditions, you may be able to follow the
river through the gap and head left once at the
base of the climbs. Access the climbs by ascending
a short piece of easy ice into a small bowl below
Eklutna Man. Follow the snow slope right to the
base of the climb. | **Descent:** V-threads for the
descent, rappel the route.

(Courtesy Michael Meyers)

8. The Nose   WI4

100m
Steve Garvey & Harry Hunt

An obvious flow to the right of *Headstone Pillars* that forms the last climb before the prow and *Mitre Might*. The first pitch tends to be thin and difficult to protect, but the ice gets better as you progress. It is possible to traverse right on the ledge before starting this climb and you will end up at the start of the crux pitch of *Mitre Might*.
| **Approach:** Same approach as *Headstone Pillars*.
| **Descent:** V-threads for the rappel.

9. Mitre Might   WI5

450m
Charlie Sassara, Mike Miller, Brian Canard & Karl Swanson, 1987

An absolute classic and stellar line. This 1000-foot expanse of ice lulls you into a sense of comfort with moderate climbing on WI3 up to a full pitch of WI5 on a pillar. Originally this line was shorter; however, climate change and a rapidly retreating Eklutna Glacier added an entire pitch at the base. The crux pitch is after 90m of enjoyable climbing to a cave this is split by lines which may form on either side. Most will descend from the top of the pillar, but continuing on will lead you into more WI3 and a snowfield. The snowfield above is a relatively low grade and does not avalanche often, although this is possible.
| **Approach:** Located on the left side of the canyon approximately 2.3 miles from Serenity Falls hut. An easy start beginning down low in the canyon. The first pitch has several variations to reach the larger upper flows. | **Descent:** V-threads for the descent. From the base of the crux pitch it is sometimes possible to walk left on the snow ledges to the base of *The Nose* and *Headstone Pillars* and then back to the valley floor.

10. Road to Nowhere   WI5

240m
Harry Hunt & Danny Kost, Feb. 1994

Road to Nowhere is located across the canyon from *Mitre Might*. When you have a route that looks

(Courtesy Harry Hunt)

(Courtesy Michael Meyers)

like it was spit from the top of the cliff, you're going to have plenty of variations on the line. The difficulty in these explain the rating, which is also highly variable depending on conditions. The main flow was first climbed by Harry Hunt and Danny Kost with the upper pillars being completed by visiting climbers from Canada, Mija and Paul Berry. Climb until reaching a large snow-covered ledge. The line splits here and any number of variations can be taken. The upper pillars only appear occasionally during a rare season. This climb is also known as *The ALCAN*. Be ready for an adventure. | **Approach:** From Serenity Falls hut head up canyon for 2.3 miles following the river. Leave the river before it constricts and head left up the slope; this can be a slog in deep snow. During the right conditions you may be able to follow the river through the gap to the upper valley. Located on the right side of the canyon. | **Descent:** Be prepared to rappel off a V-thread.

11. Freer's Tears   WI4

100m
Bob Crawford & Martin Martinez, 1988

High on the hillside, this wide pillar appears at the Bellicose-Benign Col. It was named in memory of American climber Catherine Freer, who was lost on Mt. Logan at the time of the first ascent. You have to climb up a long snow slope to reach the first pitch of ice. Be aware of snow conditions and extra cautious of wind slab. It is a classic of the area. | **Approach:** Approximately 2.75 miles from the Serenity Falls hut. Walk up valley passing *Mitre Might* on your left. Take the next small drainage on the right just past *Road to Nowhere*. This will lead you up the steep slope to the climb high on the mountainside.
| **Descent:** V-thread for the descent.

91

12. Hats Off to Herman	WI5

160m
Bob Crawford & V. Patterson

A gorgeous flow and another classic. There are plenty in this area. When this book was written it was necessary to cross or skirt the glacier to get to the base of the climb. Will it still be there in a few years? The first major flow on the left after *Mitre Might* and about a 30 minute approach from that climb. The start might require climbing on thinner ice until higher up when it thickens to a steep face. Resembles *Bridalveil Falls* in difficulty and appearance. | **Approach:** 3 miles from the Serenity Falls hut. Walk up valley after crossing the bridge until you come to the toe of the glacier. There is a steep uphill slog to get to the base of the climb from below the glacier. Skirting the glacier to the left will require the least amount of possible crevasse travel. | **Descent:** V-threads for rappel or you can traverse to the right at the top and walk down.

(Courtesy Michael Meyers)

Dane Ketner climbing next to Dance Party
during a beautiful day in the Knik Gorge
(Courtesy Michael Meyers)

KNIK RIVER VALLEY

The Knik River Valley is one of the most beautiful places to spend a day while only being a few hours from Anchorage. With possibly the greatest concentration of easily accessible ice near Anchorage, there are plenty of climbs to feel alone on even the busiest of days. When Eklutna Canyon becomes busy on the weekend, head to Hunter Creek, which has been host to several ice festivals throughout the years. If you have a snowmachine or fat bike then go into the Knik Gorge. This has become another favorite, as the approach is adventurous but not overly complicated and the climbing plus overall ambiance of the area is stellar. There are days when you'll have the entire valley to yourselves, but it is often the stopping point for many other enthusiasts who drive the road from Jim Creek Trailhead all the way to the icebergs on the glacier. We turned to see around 30 vehicles parked on the lake one day while ice climbing. Trekking to Friday Creek feels like you're exploring a hidden gem, as it takes a decent drive on a 4x4 track just to get to the mouth of the river. Overall, this is not an area to be missed.

(Image USGS The National Map: Orthoimagery)

Knik Glacier

Knik Gorge 110

Friday Creek 126

Knik River

Hunter Creek 100

Pioneer Peak 96

Eklutna Lake

Palmer

N
S

95

(Courtesy John Borland)

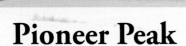

Pioneer Peak

BEER CLIMBS

Distance: 0.15 miles

Approach: 15 minutes

Difficulty: WI2 - WI4

ALERT: Access to this area crosses private property. There are posted signs to be aware of and respect. The owner is gracious enough to let climbers pass, but continue with "leave no trace" behavior to keep the access to this area open.

Access: Getting to the climbs at Pioneer Peak is relatively straightforward, as they are located just off the road. From Anchorage, drive toward Palmer on the Glenn Highway and take the turnoff for the Old Glenn Highway just before it crosses the Knik River. Instead of taking a left and heading toward Palmer, you will skirt the base of Pioneer Peak. After 7.5 miles there is a small parking area on the left side of the road. This can be easy to miss and if you get to the bridge crossing the Knik River or Knik River Road then you've gone too far.

Description: A great place for early season ice, these routes are often referred to as the Beer Climbs. While *Pilsner Pillar* may not form up as early, the two climbs on the right are more consistent. These are common early season climbs for many people due to the proximity from the car and the relatively easy nature of the climbing. There is still plenty to keep you occupied as you wait for ice season to hit full swing and even a steep, hard, mixed line that breaks off of *Pilsner Pillar* and heads to the top of the rock; steep moves and loose rock await. Other climbs exist on this flank of Pioneer with some of them going to the ridge with summit access.

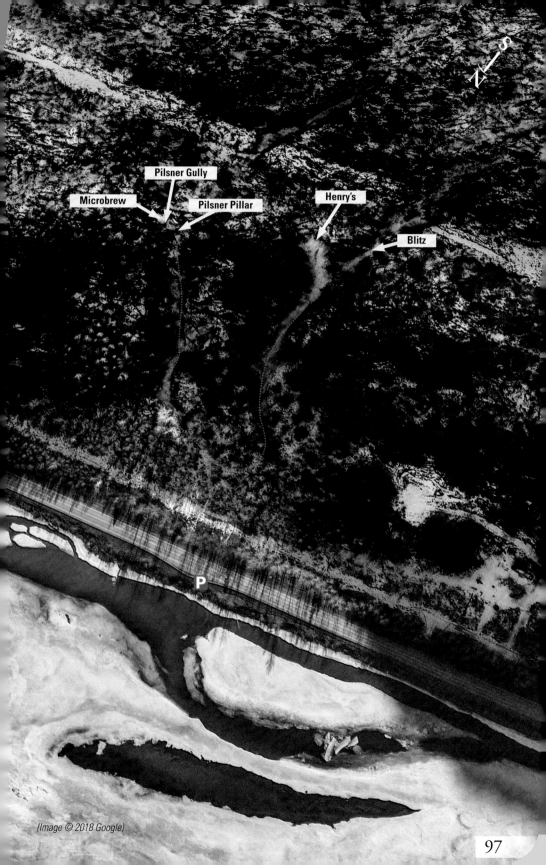

Pilsner Gully

Microbrew

Pilsner Pillar

Henry's

Blitz

P

(Image © 2018 Google)

97

(Courtesy Nathaniel Bannish)

1. Microbrew   WI4

25m

This is a small thin flow on the left side of the crag. Most of the ice is above a thick alder with thin ice below. Strangely, this climb can feel like the hardest ice in the area. Thin and difficult to protect, it doesn't always form. | **Approach:** Same start as *Pilsner Gully*. Climb left to the alder and into the small flow. Uses the same anchor as *Pilsner Gully*. | **Descent:** A large tree exists at the top of the climb above a snow slope.

2. Pilsner Gully   WI2

25m

This is an easy climb up a thin gully but it gets you to the top of *Pilsner Pillar* if you don't mind a short bushwhack. On its own it is probably not worth the hike, but can be decent as a warmup. | **Approach:** Located just to the left of *Pilsner Pillar* and climbs easy ice into the woods. | **Descent:** Large broken tree for the anchor.

The curtain below Pilsner Pillar can make a 12m wide flow that is a great place for setting up multiple ropes for beginning climbers, V-threads and screws necessary.

3. Pilsner Pillar   WI4

25m

This route can be surprisingly spicy, especially in thin conditions. Climb a short section of moderate ice to the pillar. The pillar can be good or disconnected; it all seems to depend on the year. If it is not connected, the mixed climb to get to the pillar is also surprisingly enjoyable. In addition, there is a bolted mixed line to the left. It can be hard to protect but there are usually pitons left for the pillar. | **Approach:** This route is located to the left of the next two (more popular) climbs. From the trailhead, walk toward a Private Property sign that says in small letters, "Ice Climbers Only". Head left and then take a right up the first good gully toward the ice. Awkward scrambling required and it may help to have crampons on. | **Descent:** Large tree for the anchor.

4. Henry's   WI3

50m

Conrad Guenter, B. Roberts & Steve Davis, 1984

This is probably the highest volume flow at the Beer Climbs. It almost always forms a nice large flow of easy climbing. The trail leads to a split where more ice can be seen on the right. This is the left climb that follows easy terrain up to a slightly steeper finish. A common belay point is above the large tree in the center of the photo. Scramble to below *Blitz* and then walk a small ledge left. This puts you about 30m from the top of the climb and will allow you to toprope with a 60m rope for the right side of the climb, which is usually the steeper part of the flow. | **Approach:** These climbs are in a different small drainage to the Pilsner climbs, but start on the same trail. Walk across the road and onto the trail, which may not be visible after a heavy snowfall. Continue straight instead of left and scramble through the drainage ahead up to these climbs. Be wary of hidden ice under the snow. | **Descent:** Alder bushes exist for rappel.

5. Blitz   WI2

45m

Conrad Guenter, B. Roberts & Steve Davis, 1984

From the split below *Henry's,* this climb is slightly higher and right into the woods. It is best to wear crampons for the approach as there can be a thin layer of snow over hidden ice. From the base of the ice, climb a short moderate section to a steeper short pillar. It is possible to make this climb slightly harder depending on where you climb the pillar. | **Approach:** From below *Henry's* take a right and scramble over a body-length ice step and some trees to find the start of the ice. It is best to have crampons on early. | **Descent:** From the top of the second pitch there are plenty of large trees use for the rappel. On top of the first pitch there is a large tree above dirt and rocks on the right side. This tree often has webbing hanging from it. It is not ideal for toproping with anything less than a 70m rope; be sure to tie knots in the end.

Hunter Creek

Distance: 1.3 - 2.25 miles

Approach: 20 minutes - 2 hours

Difficulty: WI2 - WI6

Access: Hunter Creek is approximately 50 miles from Anchorage and is a good day trip for some high quality climbing. From Anchorage, head north on the Glenn Highway for 30 miles before taking a right on to the Old Glenn Highway just before the bridge crossing Knik River. You do not cross the Knik River at any point heading to Hunter Creek, so it is a good marker to know if you took a wrong turn. After 8.5 miles, the road will split again. Stay right and merge on to Knik River Road, then go another 9.6 miles until you get to the bridge over Hunter Creek. The parking area is just after the bridge on the left and is usually well plowed. It can accommodate a large number of vehicles.

Description: A local favorite that has somehow remained relatively hidden from heavy exposure during the last decade. It still sees plenty of traffic, but significantly less than areas such as Eklutna Canyon or the Beer Climbs. This is partly due to the inconsistency of the river, which can make travel difficult and wet. Overland travel to the climbs further back in the drainage has existed for many years; but, due to private property restrictions, is not recommended at this time. One of those great areas that just gets better the further back you go. There are large amphitheaters and excellent testpieces that require long travel upriver and is made easier by waders or hip boots, and possibly even a raft. No matter how far you get past the first climb, you'll have a great time exploring this beautiful area.

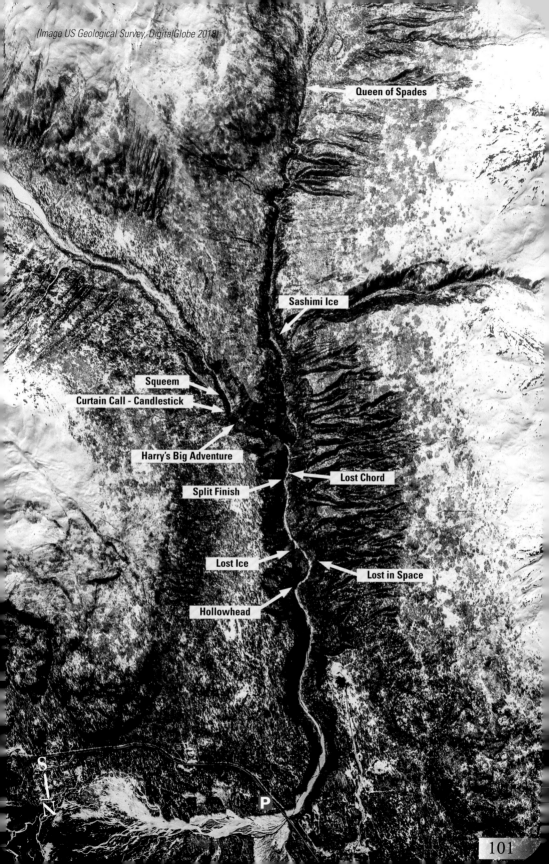

(Image US Geological Survey, DigitalGlobe 2018)

Queen of Spades

Sashimi Ice

Squeem

Curtain Call - Candlestick

Harry's Big Adventure

Split Finish

Lost Chord

Lost Ice

Lost in Space

Hollowhead

S

N

P

LOWER HUNTER CREEK

Distance: 1.3 - 2 miles

Approach: 20 - 45 minutes

Difficulty: WI3 - WI4+

ALERT: Avalanches can happen in this area. Know your surroundings and be aware of current conditions.

Access: Lower Hunter Creek describes the area from the bridge over Hunter Creek to the split between the East and West forks 2 miles into the canyon. The access to these climbs sounds a lot more straightforward than it often tends to be. Hunter Creek is a fickle river that doesn't always freeze up, leaving some interesting route-finding... with the occasional swim.

Description: Lower Hunter Creek includes some very popular ice climbs in the Southcentral area. While the approach time from Anchorage may be long compared to Eklutna Canyon, there tends to be fewer climbers and the area is beautiful. The unfortunate reality of Hunter Creek is that the river access often is the deciding factor in whether or not a climbing party will reach the ice. It does not always freeze and quite a few people have found themselves going for a swim. There are some classics in this area that make it worth the hike and the canyon has even seen a few ice festivals over the years.

1. Hollowhead	WI4+

100m
Lower Crux: Harry Hunt, Dave Lucey, & Ernie Borjon, Dec. 1995
Full Route: Ernie Borjon & Dave Lucey, Jan. 1996

Due to there being two distinct sections of this climb, it is climbed as two pitches. An easy ice flow leads into the steep 20m curtain that has spit off many strong climbers. It usually forms steep

and chandeliered and can be difficult to protect. The second pitch follows easy steps to a final 12m curtain. | **Approach:** 1.4 miles up canyon from the bridge (the first big steep flow in the canyon). It is located a hundred meters above the river and requires a hike up the steep snow/ice slope to get to the base. | **Descent:** Vegetation exists for setting up anchors.

2. Lost in Space   WI3

30m
Martin Martinez & Wayne Mushrush, 1989

A nice wide curtain after a section of moderate, easy ice. It is a good climb for beginning leaders. | **Approach:** Located just off the river, 1.5 miles from the bridge. | **Descent:** Many alder bushes are available for setting up anchors.

3. Lost Ice   WI3

60m
Ernie Borjon & Gary Bocarde, Dec. 1995

Climb a long ice gully that leads up to a curtain. The curtain may come as a surprise if you were expecting a mellow ending. It's a vertical finish to the top of the canyon. | **Approach:** 1.5 miles from the bridge. *Lost Ice* is across the canyon from

Lost in Space and, depending on snowfall, may include a steep hike up snow or a long climb off the river. | **Descent:** There is a large tree to the right of the finish, which can be used for rappel and plenty of vegetation on the way down.

4. Split Finish   WI3

150m
Dave Lucey & Harry Hunt, Dec. 1995

Fun, varied terrain that can form into steep sections interspersed with more moderate terrain. The finish is split in two giving you multiple options. A great climb for beginning leaders who want to get into longer terrain. | **Approach:** 1.94 miles from the bridge. *Split Finish* is on the left side of the river and flows right down to it. | **Descent:** Alders are available for anchors at the finish. V-thread may be necessary on the rappel.

(Courtesy Michael Meyers)   **②**   **④**   *(Courtesy Michael Meyers)*

5. Lost Chord   WI4

60m
Martin Martinez & Wayne Mushrush, 1989

This excellent climb is a must-do when in Hunter Creek. It starts with moderate climbing and then leads into a 15m pillar that provides the crux of the route. It can form into a huge flow of ice providing many fun variations and possibilities. | **Approach:** 2 miles from the bridge over Hunter Creek. Located just off the river on the right-hand side. | **Descent:** Climb up and left of the main pillar to a good tree anchor or ascend straight through the main pillar. An anchor exists below the finish to the right which allows a toprope on some thin, mixed terrain.

(Courtesy Michael Meyers)

HUNTER CREEK EAST FORK

9

Distance: 2.25 miles

Approach: 60 minutes

Difficulty: WI3 - WI6

Access: The access to this area is the same as the rest of Hunter Creek, but as the canyon thins it begins to create other obstacles. This area may require scrambling high on the hillside to navigate the open sections of the river or getting your pant legs wet. When you come to the split in the river, 2 miles from the bridge, take a left and within a short walk you will come to *Harry's Big Adventure* spilling lazily down the hillside to the river. Past *Squeem* there are additional climbs; however, the river becomes even more difficult to navigate.

Description: The East Fork of Hunter contains one of the more impressive amphitheaters in the area, known as Christmas Tree Amphitheater. Many of the routes all start off the same wide flow; there are additional routes that have been done that are not included in this guide as they don't form often. The right side of the amphitheater forms differently each year and some years it just decides to take the entire winter off. Lately it has been forming up really well and bringing these routes back into climbable shape. A trip to this area will definitely feel worth it. Only *Harry's Big Adventure* and *Squeem* are located on a different wall. Routes in the amphitheater are measured from the canyon floor to the top of the route and may include multiple lines in the measurement.

6. Harry's Big Adventure   WI3

150m
Harry Hunt & Dave Lucey, Dec. 1995

The first large flow after the split is an enjoyable moderate route up the left side of the canyon.

There are three distinct curtains and two finishes for the climb. | **Approach:** This is the first climb on the left, just after the split in Hunter Creek. It starts just off the river. | **Descent:** There are trees on top but V-threads may be necessary for additional rappels.

7. Curtain Call   WI3/4

25m
Steve Davis & Harry Hunt, 1995

There are many possible variations on this climb — most of them short, even though the height of the climb says 25m. Generally the best climbing is on the first 10-15m, with the rest being an easy jaunt up the ice slab. It is also the access point for the upper climbs and is usually climbed as such. | **Approach:** Approximately 0.2 miles from the split in Hunter Creek, continue past *Harry's Big Adventure,* and after rounding the corner, this amphitheater will be on the left. *Curtain Call* is the lower half of the wall and is the access pitch for the other climbs. | **Descent:** V-threads are necessary.

Courtesy Michael Meyers

8. Starbright   WI4

130m
Harry Hunt & Kristian Seiling, 1996

This is a really enjoyable moderate climb that gets its rating from an early crux, which leads into plenty of moderate climbing. There are ledges in the climb, but it feels like a lot of WI3 climbing over a very long pitch. This is the best climb to descend if you make it to the top of the canyon, as there is usually plenty of ice for the rappels. | **Approach:** Climb *Curtain Call* to the base of the tallest and most consistent flow, which angles left. Belay here for the start of *Starbright*. | **Descent:** Trees exist on top of the climb for the first rappel, but V-threads will be necessary for additional rappels.

9. Ornament   WI3

75m
Harry Hunt & Kristian Seiling, Jan. 1996

A short pitch leading to *Slim Jim*. Although it is considered a separate route during really stellar years, it will connect with *Slim Jim* and make one continuous climb. | **Approach:** This climb is accessed by first climbing *Curtain Call* and the first small step of *Starbright*. It is a short pitch that leads to a right-angling ramp, which heads off to *Slim Jim*.| **Descent:** V-threads for the descent, although you may have to climb further than intended to find enough ice.

10. Slim Jim   WI5

120m

This ice climb exists directly above *Ornament* and is an intimidating free-hanging pillar high on the canyon wall. There are years when it will form up really thick and connect with *Ornament* below, making a less intimidating climb, but those years are rare. Tops out when the ice runs out. | **Approach:** Climb *Curtain Call* and part of *Starbright* until next to a right-angling ledge that leads above *Ornament* to reach *Slim Jim,* or you can add *Ornament* into the mix. Belay to the left to avoid being under the pillar. | **Descent:** Alders exist at the finish. Bring V-threads for the descent. Walking left to *Starbright* at the top of the canyon and rappelling may give better options for V-threads in the middle pitches.

11. Tinsel   WI5

75m

This ice climb attacks a steep pillar of candlestick ice that is the next obvious line to the left of the *O' Christmas Tree* main pillar. | **Approach:** You have to first climb *Curtain Call* and then set up a belay near the climb. | **Descent:** Be prepared to V-thread, especially if the climb ends before the small ledge above. Alders may exist depending on conditions.

12. O' Christmas Tree   WI5

100m
Harry Hunt & Steve Davis, Dec. 1995

This line is one of the more consistent in the amphitheater, although it remains difficult. During regular years it will form into steep icicles that eventually connect with *Curtain Call*. You can start from down low or ascend the ice ramp that leads to the upper portion of the climb, which usually comes in as hanging daggers. | **Approach:** Climb *Curtain Call* to access the base of the curtain. | **Descent:** There are a few alders and trees at the top of the route but V-threads will probably be necessary.

13. Candlestick   WI6

50m
Harry Hunt & Dave Lucey, 1996

During most years this will look like a large hanging cicle that will require some mixed climbing to get to, but the really good years will make it connect all the way down. Either way it's going to be a challenge. | **Approach:** Climb the far right side of *Curtain Call* to the base of the route. | **Descent:** Getting down may be another crux depending on conditions; V-thread is likely.

14. Squeem   WI3/4

40m
Steve Davis solo, Feb. 1996

This is a relatively short climb for the area, although the ice can continue to the upper rim. It usually turns into moderate broken ice, meandering through the trees. This may form as two flows next to each other with thin ice. | **Approach:** Just after Christmas Tree

Amphitheater is another wall that includes multiple climbs. This is the first climb that spills down to the river. You may have to skirt the hillside to approach, as the river is often open beyond this point and includes many obstacles. | **Descent:** There are alders above for rappel.

HUNTER CREEK WEST FORK

Distance: 2.25 miles

Approach: 1-2 hours

Difficulty: WI2 - WI6

Access: Two miles after the bridge, Hunter Creek splits into east and west forks. The West fork is the right fork, and from here on the river opens into a new kind of adventure. There are large suspended blocks, beautiful ice gullies, and steep stout lines that pour from the canyon rim. The drainage has been explored to the end in a 6-hour one-way trip that included plenty of steep crossings and adventurous exploration. If you plan on exploring this area, it is recommended you bring some gear to stay dry in deep water (hip boots, dry suit, waders). There are usually exposed areas of the river that may make crossing difficult.

Description: The main prize is *Queen of Spades*, which is a steep WI6 that creates a beautiful series of connected pillars. There are also plenty of lines that are not included in this version of the guidebook, and potential for new lines that will hopefully make it in to future versions.

15. Sashimi Ice   WI2

200m
Ernie Borjon & Ned Lewis, Jan. 1996

A long meandering climb that winds its way up the right side canyon wall. A fun outing for some easy ice on the way to climbs further up in the canyon. | **Approach:** 2.8 miles from

(Courtesy Michael Meyers)

the bridge over Hunter Creek. Located on the right side of the canyon as you head in toward *Queen of Spades*.| **Descent:** There are trees on multiple levels of the climb for rappelling. Bring a V-thread tool just in case.

16. Queen of Spades   WI6

70m
Dave Lucey & Harry Hunt, 1997

This impressive formation creates a beautiful series of connected pillars that create a steep and difficult climb. It requires a lengthy approach and may require some swimming to get through the canyon, but if you make the trip all the way back, you will not be disappointed. Climb the series of pillars to the right in a direct line to the top. Hold on tight — it's a long ride. Best to go during extreme cold. | **Approach:** This climb is located 4.15 miles from the bridge. Follow the right split to head up Hunter Creek west. Some swimming, hip boots, packraft, or other device can be very helpful for the lengthy approach. | **Descent:** Alders for anchors and rappel, bring two ropes.

(Courtesy Michael Meyers)

Knik Gorge

38

Distance: 9 - 10 miles from road

Approach: 60 min (Snowmachine)

Difficulty: WI2 - WI6

ALERT: Water crossings are usually necessary in this area. Be wary of open water and always get out to inspect a crossing before attempting to cross it.

Access: Although it is possible to drive a truck or 4x4 to the ice when the conditions are just right, it is not always recommended. This will require a 4x4 vehicle, and you'll need to drive across the frozen lake in front of the glacier. There are often wet spots from overflow and fracture zones to be aware of; if a vehicle was to break through the ice it would be gone for the foreseeable future. Primary access on snowmachine is likely best, park at Hunter Creek and head downriver. Once at the open valley you'll need to cross Hunter Creek if you haven't already. From this point, try and follow other's tracks if you can find them, or head toward the Gorge by staying on the right side of the valley until you cross the Knik River. This area can be heavy in overflow, but traversing the river bank will hopefully bring you to an area that is frozen. Once across the Knik, stay on the left side of the river, you shouldn't have to cross it again. There is an old 4x4 road that you can occasionally pick up. Head toward the middle of the valley and, near the lake proper, there will be a moraine. Go up the moraine and down the other side. This will put you on the lake, where the climbs should be visible to the right. Head directly toward the climbs, paying attention to fractures and overflow.

Description: This area is destined to become one of the most popular areas requiring snowmachine or fatbike access, if not just for the high concentration of available ice. The area is not so much a gorge as a cliff along the side of a wide valley, but along that cliff is a several mile-long stretch of ice that could lead to over a hundred climbs. It is important to note that this area is constantly changing, not only from year-to-year, but also during each season. Climbs will form early in the season only to disappear as the ice moves to a different section of the cliff.

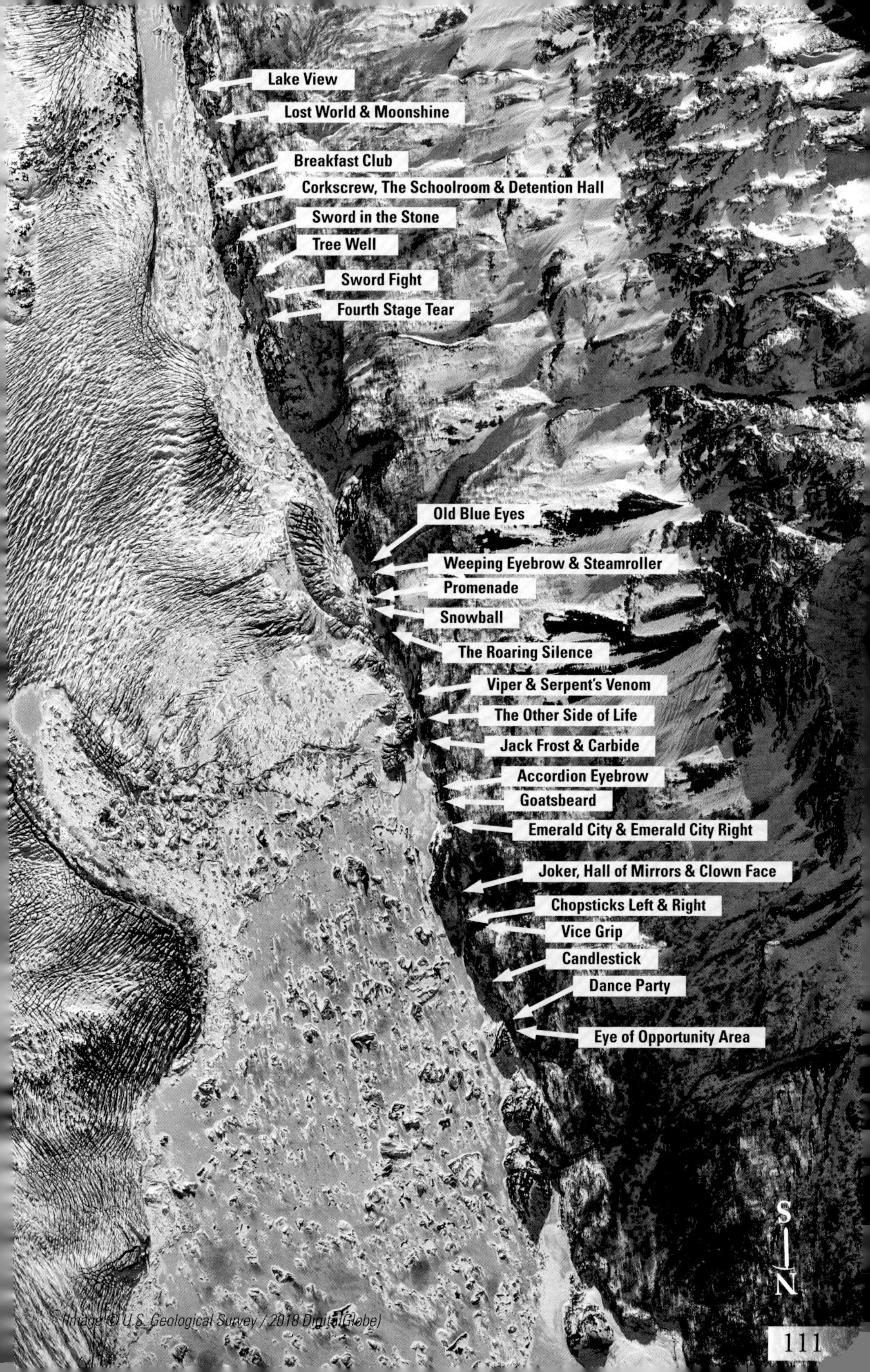
Lake View
Lost World & Moonshine
Breakfast Club
Corkscrew, The Schoolroom & Detention Hall
Sword in the Stone
Tree Well
Sword Fight
Fourth Stage Tear
Old Blue Eyes
Weeping Eyebrow & Steamroller
Promenade
Snowball
The Roaring Silence
Viper & Serpent's Venom
The Other Side of Life
Jack Frost & Carbide
Accordion Eyebrow
Goatsbeard
Emerald City & Emerald City Right
Joker, Hall of Mirrors & Clown Face
Chopsticks Left & Right
Vice Grip
Candlestick
Dance Party
Eye of Opportunity Area
S
N
(Image © U.S. Geological Survey / 2018 DigitalGlobe)

1. Lake View — WI4+

150m

Starting on a small bench, this climb goes up several steps of steep curtains then climbs a section of long, mellow ground before leading onto the upper face. | **Approach:** 3.35 miles of lake travel will get you to the base of this route, which is one of the last large ice climbs before a section of thinner climbs. | **Descent:** There is some vegetation on top but a V-thread will be necessary for additional rappels.

2. Lost World — WI4

120m

This is usually the largest flow in this area — big rolling ice with the crux at the start. A steep curtain leads up to mellow ground with many steps going into the trees. The right side of the start pitch occasionally forms into a great WI5 pillar. | **Approach:** 3.3 miles of lake travel. After the pinch, continue down the cliff until under the climb. | **Descent:** Alders on top but a V-thread will be necessary for additional rappels.

3. Moonshine — WI4

90m

A thinner climb than its neighbor to the left. This climb usually forms from a short gully and into a thicker area above. There is a 2-bolt anchor at 60m that is above the low-angle section and left

of the main upper flow; it is located in a small rock gully that heads off left. | **Approach:** 3.3 miles of lake travel. After the pinch, continue down the cliff until under the climb. | **Descent:** Alders on top and a 2-bolt anchor above the rock gully on the rock face across the low-angle section. Keep an eye for it on your way up or bring a V-thread in case you miss it.

4. Breakfast Club — WI3

40m

A surprisingly enjoyable climb that flows over several ledges, creating some small body-height pillars in several areas. This is a great climb for newer climbers. There is a bolted anchor above, but it is best to use for rappel due to its height (unless you have an 80m rope). Tie knots in the end! | **Approach:** This climb is located on the far left edge of the cliff face, and is out of view when you first enter the lake. Once you leave land and start on the lake, this route will be 3.16 miles of lake travel. | **Descent:** There is a 2-bolt anchor on top of the climb for rappel.

5. Corkscrew — WI3

30m

Part of a massive flow of ice that pours lazily over this area of the cliff. It separates into multiple climbs once it pours over the face. On the left side of the cliff is an overhanging section where the ice pours over creating some decent-sized

6. The Schoolroom   WI3

35m

The big flow in the middle of the face comes down in easy steps and has plenty of ice. Follow your own line as you make your way up to the top of the slope. A good climb for beginners. | **Approach:** Pouring directly onto the lake, this big flow will be hard to miss once you see it. Located 3.1 miles across the lake from the lake entrance. Cross the blockage gap and this climb will be the middle of the series of flows. | **Descent:** Alder bushes are available for setting up anchors at the finish. Bringing a V-thread is recommended.

7. Detention Hall   WI3

40m

The right side of the massive flow that contains the previous two climbs. It can be thin at the bottom where the ice flows over a bulge in the rock, but gets thicker in the center. Top out and rappel when the climb turns into walking. Bring screws or V-thread for the anchor on these climbs. | **Approach:** Pouring directly on to the lake, this big flow will be hard to miss once you see it. Located 3.1 miles across the lake from the lake entrance. Cross the blockage gap and this climb will be on your right-hand side. | **Descent:** V-thread necessary.

pillars. Either climb the pillar or follow the ice just to the right and continue easy climbing to the top. | **Approach:** Pouring directly onto the lake, this big flow will be hard to miss one you see it. Located 3.1 miles across the lake from the lake entrance. Cross the blockage gap and this climb will be on the left side of the flow. | **Descent:** V-threads necessary.

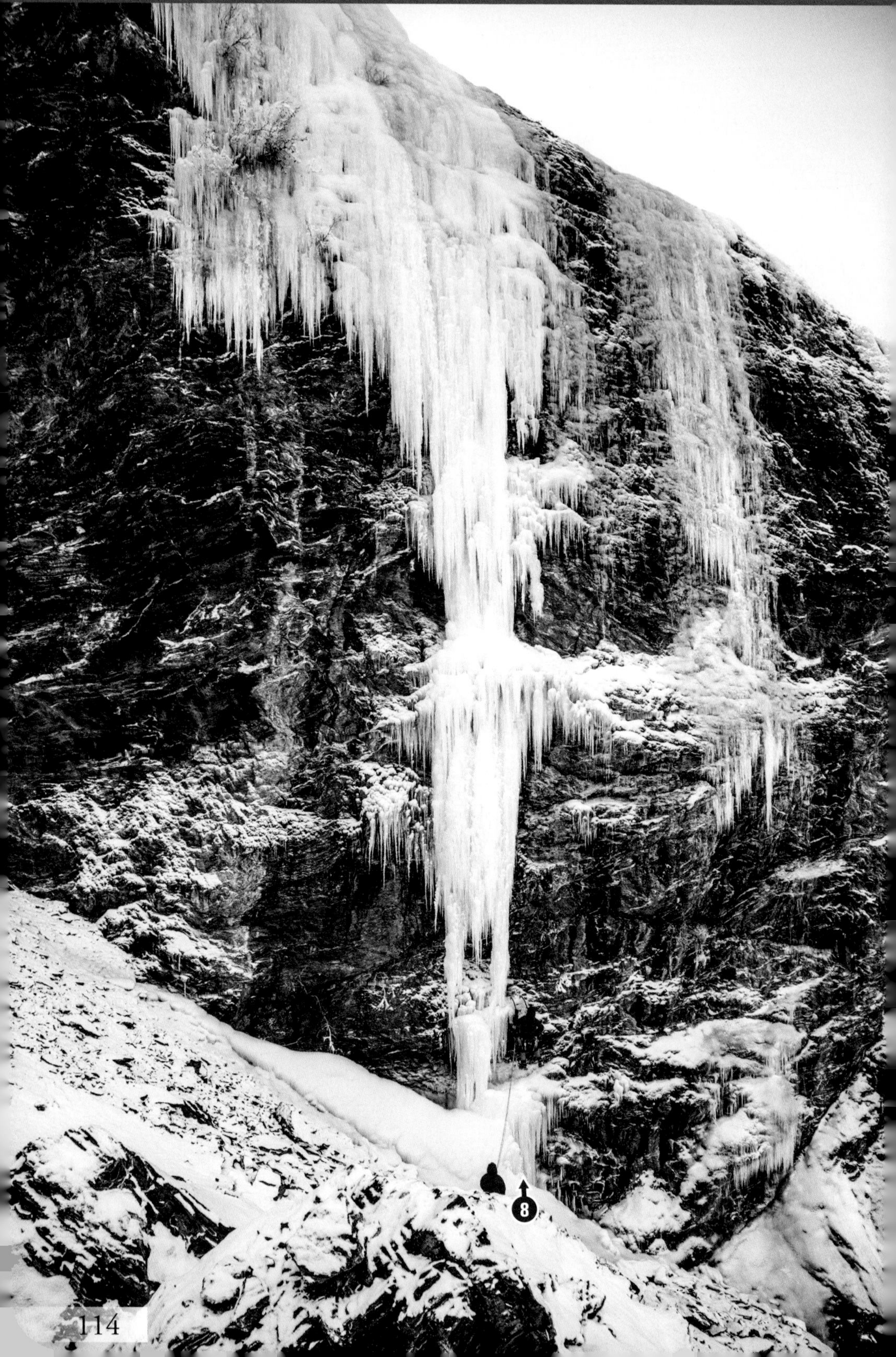
8

8. Sword in the Stone   WI6

70m
Travis Mcalpine, Mark Moeller & Tim
Stephens, 2018

An area testpiece and an absolute classic. When it is fully formed, it is probably the most impressive single piece of ice in the gorge. It was originally bolted and climbed as a mixed line, only to form up during a heavy flow year with long pillars. Travis Mcalpine got the first ascent of the mixed line (2018) with Tim Stephens nabbing the all-ice ascent (2019). The bolts were clipped on both ascents. There is an anchor at the top of the first pitch just above a ledge on the left side of the pillars. Continue more hard climbing to a 2-bolt anchor above. There is also a pin and a bolt on the second pitch, but these may be buried depending on conditions. | **Approach:** 2.97 miles from the lake entrance. Just after the amphitheater for *First Stage Tear*. This climb is in its own gully that faces left. | **Descent:** Bolted anchors exist at the top, as well as a lower anchor for rappel.

9. Tree Well   WI3

180m

This line flows over steps as it makes its way lazily down into the amphitheater. It may require some easy climbing to get to the base, but often only requires a hike up the snow ramp. | **Approach:** 2.75 miles from the lake entrance. Located at the gap, where it is common to climb over a small rock band to get to the climbs on the other side. It is in the same amphitheater as *First Stage Tear*. | **Descent:** Alders exist on top for the first rappel. V-threads will be necessary for additional rappels.

10. Sword Fight   WI5

35m
Tim Stephens & Travis Mcalpine, 2019

This line doesn't always form, but when it does, it pours down the prow of a small rock cliff forming a series of connected pillars. | **Approach:** 2.75 miles from the lake entrance. Located at the gap, where it is common to climb over a small rock band to get to the climbs on the other side. This is in an amphitheater to the left of *First Stage Tear*. | **Descent:** Alders exist on top for the rappel.

11. Fourth Stage Tear   WI5

70m
Matt Peters, Josué Wulf & John Giraldo,
Feb. 2018

At the time of printing this guide, there is an area where the glacier constricts against the rock cliff; this is usually as far as you can go on snowmachine. You then have to do a short scramble over the rock to get to the other side of the constriction where more climbs await. In the middle of the constriction, a decent-sized amphitheater opens up. This is the most obvious piece of ice on the wall, with several pillars connecting to the base. Connect the pillars using a variety of gear; don't forget your small screws (the first ascent party suggests pitons). | **Approach:** 2.75 miles across the lake is an area where the glacier is the closest to the cliff, at least in 2018. This is where the climb is located: in a small amphitheater a few hundred feet off the glacier. | **Descent:** V-threads necessary for rappel.

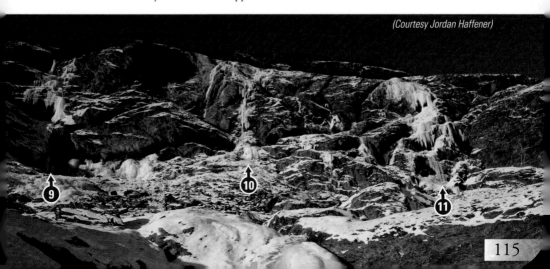

(Courtesy Jordan Haffener)

12. Old Blue Eyes	**WI4**

45m
Martin Martinez & Jeff Jablonski, Feb. 1999

An area of the gorge where there are plenty of ice lines to be found. This is the first line on the left that is shorter than *Weeping Eyebrows* and *Steamroller* but still a great line. Start on a wide curtain of hanging ice and continue steep climbing until above the pillar. Easy climbing to the left will get you to the alders above. | **Approach:** 2.15 miles from the lake entrance. Approach along the cliff. This climb is located to the left of a much larger flow of ice that combines to make the next two climbs. | **Descent:** There are some alders/trees but a V-thread may also be helpful.

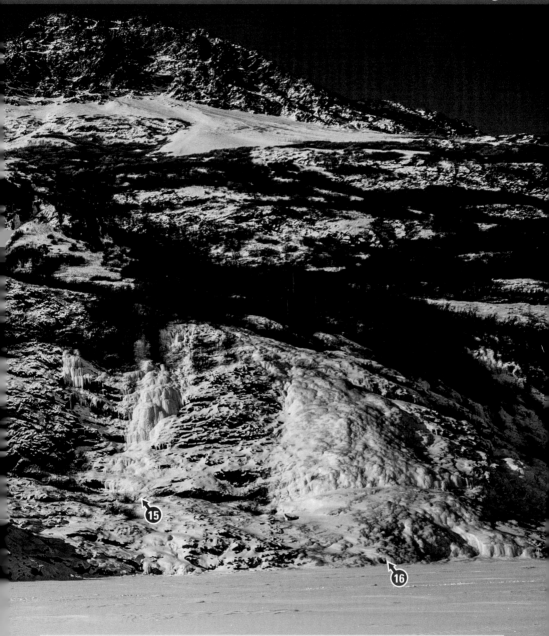

13. Weeping Eyebrow   WI3

50m
Martin Martinez & Jeff Jablonski, Feb. 1999

The left of two lines that start on an often connected flow. It is said that this flow usually runs all winter and that it can be a good place to get drinking water. The upper half of the climb may be thin with water running behind. Once above the first curtain, stay left to follow an ever thinning ice band.

| **Approach:** 2.15 miles from the beginning of the lake. Left of a large, heaving pile of ice called *Snowball*. | **Descent:** Alders and V-threads for the rappel.

14. Steamroller   WI4

60m
Martin Martinez & Jeff Jablonski, Feb. 1999

Start on an often thick curtain of deep blue ice
that thins after the first pillar until the top. There
are several different variations on the upper
section that can be done, and most end before
the top of the cliff where the vegetation awaits.
There may be a few feet of mossy mixed climbing
to reach the alders. | **Approach:** 2.15 miles from
the beginning of the lake, left of a large heaving
pile of ice called *Snowball*. | **Descent:** Alders and
V-threads for the rappel.

15. Promenade   WI3-

60m
Jeff Jablonski & Martin Martinez

A nice, long climb that can be great for beginner
climbers or as a warmup. There are not a lot
of WI2 or WI3- climbs in this guide that are
listed for this area, so get them where you can.
Promenade is just to the left of *Snowball* slightly
higher off the lake. Ramp right with plenty of ice
into the vegetation above. | **Approach:** 2.1 miles
from the beginning of the lake, left of *Snowball*.
| **Descent:** Alders and V-threads for the rappel.

16. Snowball   WI2

80m

Snowball is a hard climb to miss. It is a giant
spread of ice that has plenty of variations for
beginner climbers. It would make a good first
ice lead or place to set up multiple ropes for
beginners. Pick your path and head on up.
| **Approach:** Approximately 2.1 miles from the
beginning of the lake. Look for a large heap of ice
that appears to cover an entire knoll. | **Descent:**
V-threads for the descent.

17. The Roaring Silence   WI4-

80m

Located in a small alcove that can protect
climbers from a heavy wind. What looks like a
rock wall with a few hanging icicles is actually a
flow that comes down in a small five-meters-wide
canyon. This area is identifiable by a curtain of
large hanging cicles and a small moraine that

blocks the base of the wall. You have to hike
around the moraine to get to the base. The right
side of this small canyon is called *The Roaring
Silence*. This climb heads up into a forest with
plenty of anchors. | **Approach:** 2 miles from the
start of the lake. Located in a small canyon that
requires you to hike over a moraine. The top of
the climbs may be visible; a defining feature is a
few large hanging cicles nearly hidden from view.
| **Descent:** The top has plenty of vegetation for
anchors but a V-thread may be necessary for a
second rappel.

18. Viper   WI5

50m
Travis Mcalpine & Pat Schmalix, Feb. 2018

From afar, this route looks like the separation in
a viper's tongue. Climb two separated daggers for
the start of the route and then lead into thicker
yet still steep ice above. | **Approach:** Mile 1.8
from the beginning of the lake. This route and
Serpent's Venom are several hundred meters left
of *The Other Side of Life*. Hike over a small rock
band toward the face shaped like a diamond to
the base of the route. | **Descent:** There is a tree
anchor to the left of the top of the climb.

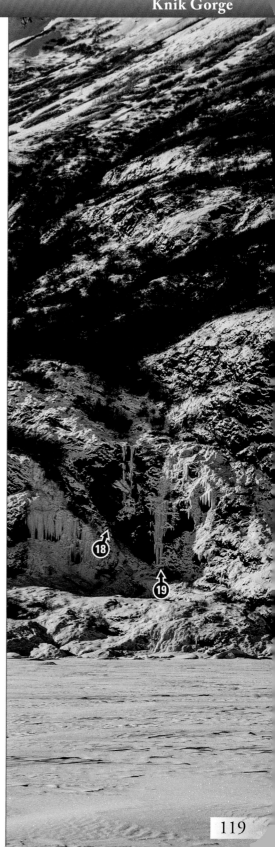

19. Serpent's Venom   WI5

50m

Travis Mcalpine & Josué Wulf, Feb. 2018

Part of the new generation of Knik Gorge routes. This one follows what looks like two small drips high on a cliff. Climb a wild, thin pillar using mostly rock gear for protection. This may require additional mixed climbing down low due to thin ice at the start. | **Approach:** 1.8 miles from the beginning of the lake. Located on a rock face that is shaped like a diamond from the side. Hike over a small rock band and then traverse the ramp on the left to the base of the route. | **Descent:** There are trees on top that can be used for rappel.

20. The Other Side of Life   WI4-

90m

Martin Martinez & Dave Hart, Feb. 1999

This long flow is just left of *Jack Frost* and *Carbide*, it goes to just below the upper tree line. The first ascent was done in -30 degree temps, for those who want to emulate the feeling of the first ascent and don't mind torture. Climb easy ice to a thick, steeper band that then eases off back to WI3. | **Approach:** 1.74 miles from the beginning of the lake and located in a large concentration of ice. This is the longest flow on this section of the wall leading from the lake to the top of the cliff. | **Descent:** Alders exist on the top and near the lower third of the route, but a V-thread may be necessary depending on rope length.

21. Jack Frost   WI3+

90m

Jeff Jablonski & Martin Martinez

During the later part of the season, this may look like a single wide section of ice; however, the left side is often slower to form and may not be in, even though *Carbide* is ready. When formed, it is often thin with a rocky start that thickens in the middle. Follow the ice as it veers left until the alder finish. The first ascent of this climb was done in a single rope length with winds at 40mph, creating a whiteout for Jablonski. | **Approach:** Mile 1.7 from the start of the lake. Starts just off the lake up a small rock ramp. | **Descent:** A large alder ledge traverses the top of the climb. V-thread for the second rappel.

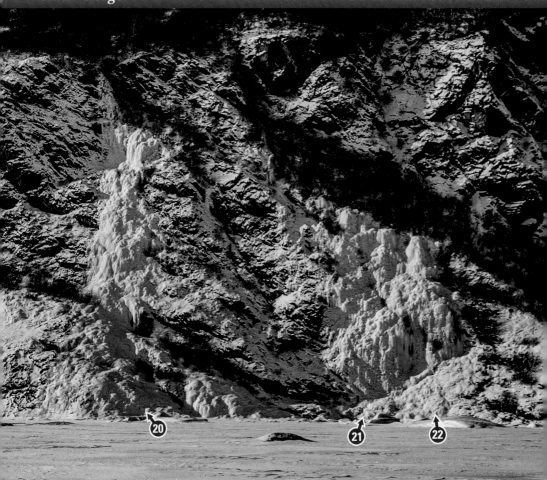

22. Carbide	WI4

60m
Martin Martinez & Jeff Jablonski

Carbide is the more obvious portion of ice in this band. It follows a steep and continuous flow that leads to the upper alders. There is a variation in the middle where a small cave forms, leaving the option of going left or right at the cave.
| **Approach:** Mile 1.7 from the start of the lake. This climb and the next may form one solid band of ice during a good season. Climb the right side of the flow that ends in a downward, right-sloping tree ledge. | **Descent:** A large ledge of alders traverses the top of the climb. Bring a V-thread tool for a possible second rappel.

23. Accordion Eyebrow	WI4

65m
Travis Mcalpine & Michael Briseno, 2019

Another fickle line that doesn't fully form as often as some of the surrounding climbs, as the picture on the opposite page shows. This climb is often nearly non-existent while the surrounding lines are fat and healthy. The first pitch is even less consistent, but it is a quality line when in. The first pitch leads to a ramp before the second pitch. The ice tends to be thin on this line, which may make protection difficult. | **Approach:** 1.6 miles from the beginning of the lake. Scramble to the base. | **Descent:** A Spectre exists for the anchor; bring a V-thread just in case.

24. Goatsbeard   WI3

55m

This climb is just barely separate from the rest of *Emerald City,* but is an enjoyable climb in its own right. It is just left of the *Emerald City* mass and requires a bit of scrambling to get to the base. | **Approach:** Mile 1.5 from the start of the lake. Head toward the biggest chunk of ice on the horizon and it will probably be *Emerald City. Goatsbeard* is just to the left. | **Descent:** Alders and V-threads.

25. Emerald City   WI3+

140m
Martin Martinez & Jeff Jablonski, 1998

One of the most impressive pieces of ice in the gorge. Nearly 60 meters wide at the bottom it feels like you've entered a city of ice when you pull up to it. There are many possibilities along the face with a long pillar finish to get to the top of the right pinnacle. Picking the easiest path through the climb will give you a grade of WI3+ during good conditions. You can choose your own adventure to up the difficulty. | **Approach:** 1.5 miles from the beginning of the lake. Look for the largest chunk of ice on the cliff. This is probably going to be *Emerald City*. | **Descent:** There are some alders but V-threads will likely be necessary.

26. Emerald City Right   WI4

140m

This is a long and steep flow next to *Emerald City*; a flow of connected ice on the right side that can be climbed to the top. The ice flow is about 60m, but requires easy climbing to get to the base, making the route much longer. Martin Martinez and John Weiland climbed it in 1998, believing they may be on the first ascent, when they found webbing at the top. A common occurrence in Alaska, where you never know who might have been there before you. | **Approach:** 1.5 miles from the beginning of the lake. Look for the largest chunk of ice on the cliff. This is probably going to be *Emerald City*; look to the right for this climb. | **Descent:** There are some alders but V-threads will be necessary.

121

27. Joker   WI3

15m

A fun line that can be a great place to escape the wind or enjoy a fun day climbing moderate lines right next to each other. A thick enjoyable flow. | **Approach:** 1.25 miles on the lake will get you to the *Chopsticks*. This line and the next two are located in a small area up and to the left of the *Chopsticks*. It requires a long pitch of WI2 to get to this amphitheater. Some parties may want to rope up for portions of this pitch. Once in the amphitheater, this climb is on the far left. | **Descent:** Alders exist for the rappel.

28. Hall of Mirrors   WI3

20m

This line can form into strange, broken sections below due to the way the rock at the bottom redirects the water. Fun climbing on strange ground leads you to a steeper face before the finish. | **Approach:** Same as *Joker*. This is the middle climb. | **Descent:** Alders exist for the rappel.

29. Clown Face   WI3+

25m

The right climb in this small amphitheater proved to be a fun and engaging challenge. The anchor (solid trees) tends to be pretty far back from the lip, but there are smaller bundles near top of the ice. The height of this route is made longer by the anchor distance. | **Approach:** Same as *Joker*; this is the right line. | **Descent:** Alders exist for rappel.

30. Chopsticks Left   WI4

60m
Martin Martinez, Richard Baranow & Wendy Sanem, Dec. 1997

These lines are to the right of *Emerald City* and around the rock bend. The *Chopsticks* are the two independent ice lines separated by a rock band in the middle but connected at the top. *Chopsticks* left climbs the left flow that is often thin at the bottom but gets fatter in the middle. | **Approach:** 1.25 miles on the lake will get you to the *Chopsticks*. They are just to left of *Vice Grip*. | **Descent:** Alders and V-threads.

The photo shows Candlestick and the several pillars that lead up to the main pitch, enjoyable in their own right.

31. Chopsticks Right WI4

50m

Jeff Jablonski & Martin Martinez, 1998

The right of the two *Chopsticks*. This line is usually thinner than its counterpart and ends at the base of a ramp, with alders for the belay. | **Approach:** 1.25 miles on the lake will get you to the *Chopsticks*, two popular aesthetic climbs. They are just to left of a small canyon that holds another climb called *Vice Grip*. | **Descent:** Alders exist at the top.

32. Vice Grip WI3

60m

Martin Martinez, Richard Baranow & Wendy Sanem, Dec. 1997

Depending on where you are standing, this climb may be entirely hidden from view. It is tucked away in the back of a small canyon just to the right of the *Chopsticks*. Scramble into the canyon and head up the back of the chimney filled with ice. | **Approach:** 1.25 miles on the lake will get you to the *Chopsticks* and this hidden route. It is often hard to see until you are past the climb or at the base. Find the climb hidden in the small canyon. | **Descent:** Vegetation exists on top for anchors.

33. Candlestick WI5

30m

Travis Mcalpine & Pat Schmalix, Feb. 2018

At first glance, the *Candlestick* looks like just a small smear on the rock, which it is; but that doesn't mean it didn't get climbed. Climb one of the two pillars below (WI4) and then walk to the base of the *Candlestick*. There may be some rock moves required to get onto the climb and then a few more when you reach it. Top out on the easy ice above and find a few alders in the flow. | **Approach:** 1.1 miles from the beginning of the lake. Approach by heading directly toward the cliff and then traverse until you find the small smear hanging from a baby rock amphitheater. It sits above a ledge. | **Descent:** There are a few alders for a rappel but be prepared for a V-thread just in case.

34. Dance Party WI3+

40m

This area of the gorge is becoming a local favorite, as it has impressive ice and some high-quality mixed lines. The ice in this area may be formed by the water moving away from the *Eye of Opportunity* area, which has created some great lines. This is the only consistent, continuous ice line that forms on this wall. Traverse left following the ice as it leads to a flat ledge above. More ice continues above this section, but this is the most common place to anchor and rappel. | **Approach:** 1 mile from the start of the lake. This line and the others in the area are all located in a small alcove that is mostly hidden from view when seen from the lake. There is a small moraine that you have to hike around to reach these climbs and they are the first climbs in the Gorge from the approach. | **Descent:** There are alders, but a V-thread is also a good idea if you are going to use one rope or toprope.

35. Eye of Opportunity WI5

45m

Steve Garvey, Martin Martinez & Eddie Phay, 1996

You may look at this wall and only see rocks, wondering where the ice lines are supposed to be, or you can get lucky and the water will flow over the cliff. This flow seems to meander from year-to-year, but these were some of the original lines in the gorge. This is a steep line that ascends a pillar through the overhang, that does not always connect to the ground. It is an excellent stout climb when it is in. Continue left of the middle cave and top-out at the alders. | **Approach:** Same as *Dance Party*. This line should be right in front of you when you approach up the slope. | **Descent:** Alders exist on top.

36. Three Amigos   WI4+

42m
Steve Garvey, Martin Martinez & Eddie Phay, 1996

The middle of three lines that are close together in the alcove (see *Eye of Opportunity*). Follow to the right of the cave on this steep line. | **Approach:** This line and the others in the area are all located in a small alcove that is mostly hidden from view when seen from the lake. There is a small moraine that you have to hike around to reach these climbs — they are the first climbs in the gorge from the approach. | **Descent:** Alders exist on top.

The image below may look strange considering there are route markers that point up the rock face instead of an ice route. This area changes from year-to-year and these lines don't always form, but when they do they are high quality lines. They are also some of the original climbs that were done in the gorge with first ascents by Steve Garvey and Eddie Phay: two local legends who left us too soon.

37. Happy Daze   WI3

30m
Steve Garvey, 1996

This was first climbed as a solo by Steve Garvey to take pictures during the first ascent of the climbs in this small amphitheater. The right of three lines that can be connected in the middle. Follow to the right and top-out between rock faces. | **Approach:** This line and the others in the area are all located in a small alcove that is mostly hidden from view when seen from the lake. There is a small moraine that you have to hike around to reach these climbs; they are the first climbs in the gorge from the approach. | **Descent:** Alders exist on top for rappel.

38. Overflow   WI4

30m
Martin Martinez & Eddie Phay 1996

Another climb located over the small moraine that leads to the previous climbs. Climbed during a one-day push that saw four new first ascents in this area. | **Approach:** This line and the others in the area are all located in a small alcove that is mostly hidden from view when seen from the lake. There is a small moraine that you have to hike around to reach these climbs; they are the first climbs in the gorge from the approach. | **Descent:** Many alder bushes are available for setting up anchors.

Friday Creek

6

Distance: 1.24 - 3.5 miles

Approach: 30 minutes - 1.5 hours

Difficulty: WI2 - WI4+

Access: To get to Friday Creek, take the Glenn Highway north from Anchorage. After going past Eklutna, exit at the Old Glen Highway just before the Knik River Bridge. Turn right and begin heading east adjacent to the Knik River. After several miles, the main road will curve left and cross the Knik River. Once over the bridge, turn right on Sullivan Avenue, then right again into Jim Creek Recreational Area. This is a large parking lot. Follow the trail on the east edge as it makes its way through the trees and to the river after 1 mile. Continue on the left edge of the river, crossing several channels. The trail may head back into the trees within a few miles of Friday Creek; these will often try to skirt thinner sections of the river. The crux of the drive usually comes near the end where it crosses several deeper river sections that may not freeze. Depending on the height of your vehicle, you may be able to drive through it or skirt it with a snowmachine. Once on the river head, into the canyon. Approach times vary greatly with the type of transportation and conditions of the approach trail. Mile descriptions for each approach are measured from parking near the entrance to the canyon.

Description: Friday Creek is relatively hidden compared to the other areas listed for Knik River Valley. Most people will have never seen or crossed this stream, as the only way to access it is through a 9 mile 4x4 trail. It is located directly across the valley from Hunter Creek and follows a stream into a valley that is a relatively deep drainage. Despite its perceived difficulty in access, it is under-appreciated; there are several high-quality climbs in a beautiful, quiet area. The canyon winds for miles, but most will stop after *Octave* as it is the prize of the area. For those willing to travel, several other climbs await, with potential for more exploration further in. River crossings are likely; bring extra boots or a way to keep your feet dry.

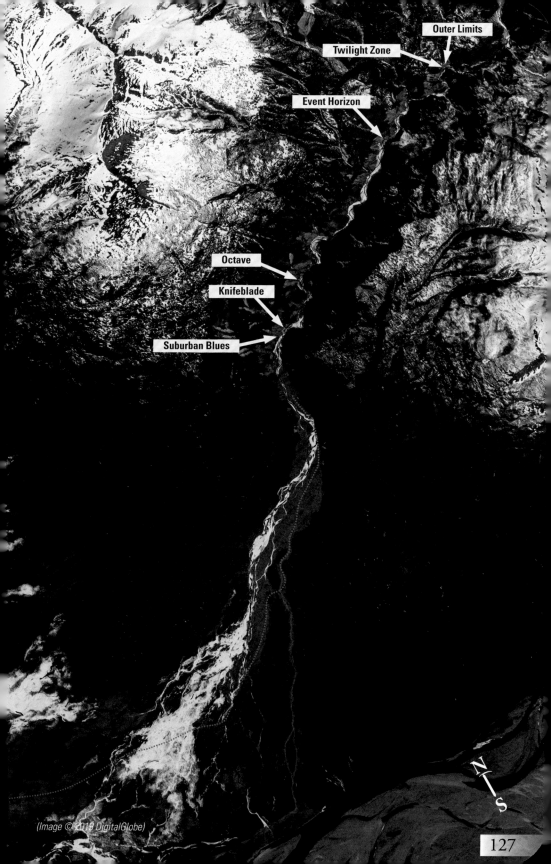

Outer Limits

Twilight Zone

Event Horizon

Octave

Knifeblade

Suburban Blues

N
S

(Image © 2019 DigitalGlobe)

1. Suburban Blues　　　　WI2

60m

The first good flow on the left side of the river. A decent, thick flow that is a good warmup before heading to *Octave*. | **Approach:** 1.24 miles up Friday Creek. Located just off the left side of the river right before *Knifeblade*. | **Descent:** Trees exist for descent at multiple levels of the climb.

2. Knifeblade　　　　　　WI4+

35m
Martin Martinez, Dec. 1993

A small smear that doesn't appear every year. *Knifeblade* was given its name because they used Knifeblades on the first ascent. Remember to bring some rock gear if you plan on climbing this line, as it is usually thin when it does appear. | **Approach:** 1.25 miles up Friday Creek. This climb is on the left-hand side, although during dry years it may not be in. | **Descent:** There is a tree anchor that can be used to rappel with a single rope, though you may need to downclimb the last few meters. Bring a V-thread just in case.

3. Octave　　　　　　　　WI4

75m
Martin Martinez, 1993

This climb is the prize of Friday Creek, and during thick flow years, may form additional ice lines on both sides. Located on the left side of the canyon, this great climb starts steep at the rim and then flows into a wide fan at the base. Start on mellow ground and then lead into steep climbing with small pillars to finish. | **Approach:** Located 1.5 miles up Friday Creek. This is the first good flow that you come to on the approach. | **Descent:** There are trees on multiple levels of the climb that should be adequate for rappels. Bring a V-thread for backup.

4. Event Horizon　　　　WI3

50m

A mile upriver from *Octave,* this climb pours from the left side of the canyon. A fun consolation prize if you don't make it all the way back to *Twilight Zone.* Follow the line direct to a large fallen tree above, which forms the anchor. There is additional ice above this pitch after a

(Courtesy Michael Meyers)

(Courtesy Michael Meyers)

short climb up a snow ramp. | **Approach:** 2.5 miles up Friday Creek on the left-hand side of the river. This climb is around a bend and before a left-hand gully that leads into a mini canyon. | **Descent:** Large trees exist on the upper rim of the canyon for rappel.

5. Twilight Zone   WI3

50m
Martin Martinez & Lawley, 1994

Two miles upriver from *Octave,* this climb pours from the left side of the canyon. Climb easy ground to a steeper upper section and then into the trees. | **Approach:** 3.4 miles up Friday Creek on the left-hand side of the river. This climb is around a large bend after a thin left-hand gully that leads into a mini canyon. | **Descent:** Large trees on the upper rim of the canyon for rappel.

6. Outer Limits   WI3

50m
Martin Martinez & Lawley, 1994

Just past *Twilight Zone* is another flow that comes down from the canyon rim on the left-hand side. It forms a thick drip to the left of the main flow that can be climbed if the direct start is less formed. Continue through a lightly meandering climb to the top. | **Approach:** 3.5 miles up Friday Creek. Pass *Twilight Zone* and look for this flow on the left. | **Descent:** Trees exist on the upper rim of the canyon.

(Courtesy Michael Meyers)

Leo Anders leading Hillside Pillar Right

MATANUSKA RIVER VALLEY

The Matanuska River Valley may require more of a time commitment to most Anchorage folks; it takes hours behind the wheel to get close to the multitude of options. But, what it may lack in accessibility, it offers up excellent early and late season conditions. This area can often see temperatures that plummet to single digits, and much lower in the dead of winter. This cold is a necessity to access many of the climbs using frozen rivers where routes line canyon walls. Brave the cold, or better yet, just watch for a break in the weather after things have set up. But if you just can't wait, areas like Caribou Creek offer an early season venue with classics like *Kid's Corner*, accessible by river access or walking in to the top if the river is not frozen yet. If you are patient, other areas like Boulder or Gravel Creek provide the ultimate backcountry experience with big routes and little climbing traffic.

Caribou Creek 150

Matanuska Glacier

Glacier Creek 146

①

Purinton Creek 142

Gravel Creek 144

Boulder Creek 138

Chickaloon

Hatcher Pass 134

③

Palmer

N
S

(Image © Google Earth, Landsat / Copernicus)

Hatcher Pass

Distance: 0.4 miles

Approach: 30 - 45 min

Difficulty: WI3 - WI3+

ALERT: Avalanches can and will happen in this area. Know your surroundings and be aware of current conditions.

Access: These climbs are located 50 miles from Anchorage on Hatcher Pass Road, 2.5 miles past the Little Susitna Bridge on the way toward Independence Mine. The best parking is currently at Skeetawk Ski Area, just down the road from the climbs, but make sure not to block any entrances. It is recommended that you park before the gate, as it closes at 5pm. The best parking used to be at a pullout just off the road directly below the gully for Hillside Pillars, but recently people have been receiving tickets for parking on the road. If this pullout is plowed, then it is still probably the best place to park. Hillside Pillars are consistently forming pillars located halfway up the mountainside and offer excellent WI3-4 toproping and lead opportunities. Getting to the base of the pillars is a whole other challenge that makes for an even better day in the outdoors. Begin this route on WI2-3 ice that snakes through a narrow ravine up to a shorter, yet steeper section. It is best to put crampons on early, as there is plenty of ice under the snow on the approach and it can get dangerous quickly. Keep your ice tools handy, as you'll be using them on the approach to the base of the main climbs.

Description: Hatcher Pass is a beautiful area that provides recreation in all seasons. Excellent rock climbing gives way to amazing skiing and mountains that will provide challenges at all difficulties. There are only a few easily accessible ice climbs in Hatcher Pass. Hatcher's climbs are located on the mountainside near the lower end of the valley before the steep rise up toward Independence Mine. *Hillside Pillars* can be busy on the weekend with several parties vying for space.

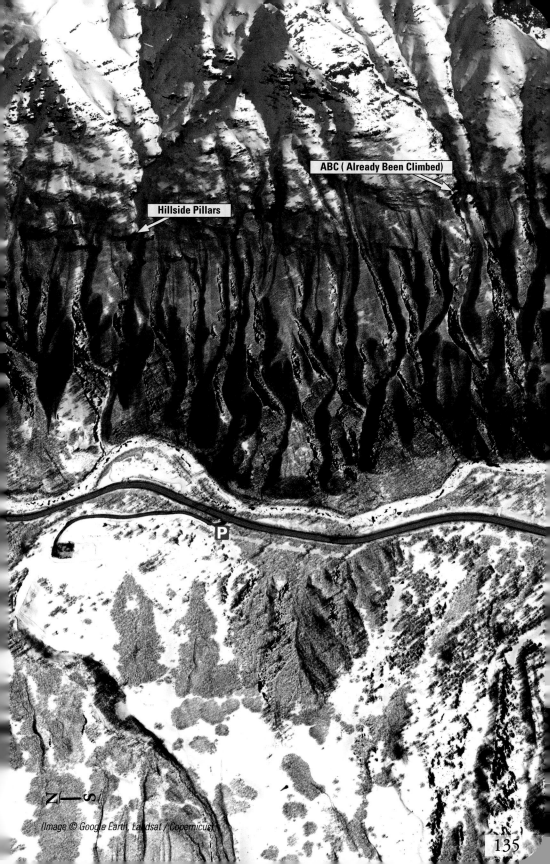

Hillside Pillars

ABC (Already Been Climbed)

P

N—S

(Image © Google Earth, Landsat / Copernicus)

135

1. Hillside Pillars Left Side   WI3

25m
Rik Derrick & Micky Hill, 1978

The left climb is the more sustained of the two and heads through a small canyon constriction up high. A worthwhile pitch of ice that is an enjoyable climb. There are bolts that head right from this climb into the corner above for a mixed line. *Mixed Route (M5):* Between the two main ice pitches exists a bolted mixed route. Access the dihedral by climbing up the right side of *Hillside Pillar Left* and traverse onto the route. From there, several bolts will take you up to an alder anchor. | **Approach:** Once in the small bowl, this is the climb on the left. | **Descent:** There is a new 2-bolt anchor on top of the route, as well as trees. It is best to use the bolted anchor, as continuing to use the trees can eventually damage them.

Hillside Pillars viewed from the parking lot. The short approach pitches can be seen leading up to the main flow

2. Hillside Pillars Main Falls   WI3+

30m
Rik Derrick & Micky Hill, 1978

Depending on where you decide to climb, this it could be as easy as WI3+ or as hard as you want it to be. During early season or low flow conditions, there is some fun mixed climbing in the small cave on the first pillar. | **Approach:** The main section of ice directly in front of the approach trail. | **Descent:** Many alder bushes are available for setting up anchors.

3. ABC (Already Been Climbed) WI3+

25m

On most years, this climb forms a very thin free-hanging curtain. As such, it receives the more difficult rating in these conditions. However, during a wet season, this climb can form a relatively easy line. A short section of WI2 ice leads to more vertical ice that ends just above the notch in the rock face. | **Approach:** Similar to the more popular neighbor, *Hillside Pillars*, this route is located on the right and about halfway up the mountainside (as seen when driving north from Palmer). Parking immediately below the route is possible if enough room is available on the shoulder of the road, but you may get ticketed. Best access is currently at Skeetawk Ski Area. Cross the river and hike either of the two ravines, which will take you to the base of the route. | **Descent:** Rappel using alders or V-thread.

Boulder Creek

(Courtesy Matthew Tucker)

Distance: 9 - 25 miles

Approach: 1 - 3 hours (snowmachine)

Difficulty: WI3 - WI5

ALERT: Avalanches are common in this area, with both the climbs and the approach being avalanche prone. Be wary of this area in poor conditions or heavy snow.

Access: The best access for this area is by snowmachine or a fast team of skiers. If you're going to go human powered, then spending the night is definitely going to be the best bet for most of the climbs — the first, *Taurine Scream*, is 9 miles from the trailhead. Located 90 miles from Anchorage. Drive towards Palmer. Pass through Palmer and continue on the Glenn Highway toward Matanuska Glacier. Park at the Purinton Creek Trailhead

(mile 90.7). There are several entrances to the trails that lead to this area, which is the most defined and has the most parking. These trails are used by motorized traffic, that may put down a good trail. Follow the trails toward the mountain and then head left as it goes towards Boulder Creek. There are plenty of off-shoot trails on this area, but try to head toward the Boulder Creek Drainage at an angle. Head into the drainage after rounding the large bend. There are many drainages in this area and GPS coordinates can be helpful. They are located in the index of this book.

Description: It can get really cold in these valleys and Boulder Creek is no exception. It takes at least a 9-mile ride to get here, and you'll probably be alone on these great climbs. *Big Bubbler* and *Superstition* form in large masses, while *Boulder Creek Pillars* makes for an amazing trip, with steep sustained pillars for the prize. Unfortunately, prizes can often come with a price; these pillars are usually still dripping, creating a wet and wild experience.

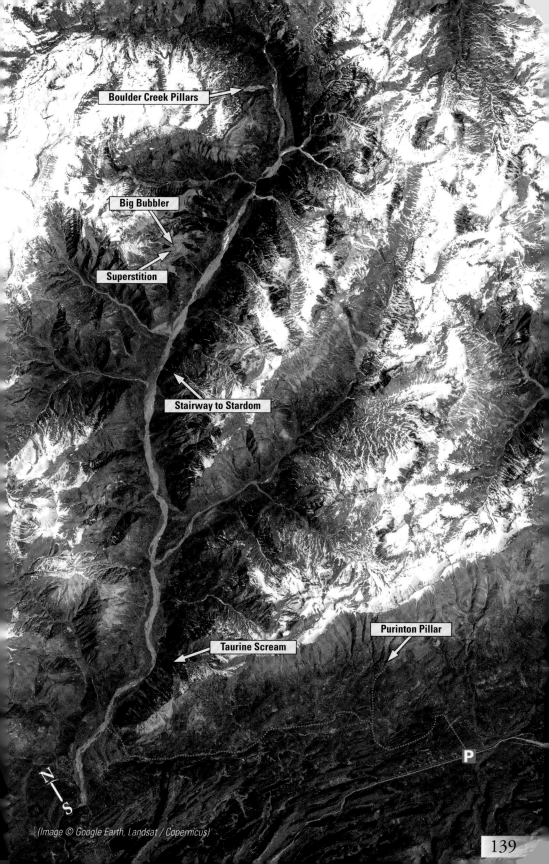

Boulder Creek Pillars

Big Bubbler

Superstition

Stairway to Stardom

Taurine Scream

Purinton Pillar

N
S

P

(Image © Google Earth, Landsat / Copernicus)

1. Taurine Scream — WI5

50m
Dave Lucey & Mike Miller, 2004

The first climb on the long approach up Boulder Creek. This climb, depending on how direct you approach, is around 9 miles from the trailhead. You won't be able to completely tell if the pillar is touching the ground unless you hike to the base, so it does take some level of commitment, and the pillar isn't known to touch down often. Most parties will continue up river to find the larger flows. | **Approach:** Approximately 9 miles in from the trailhead, this climb is the first good flow. It will be located on the right side of the river 1.25 miles after the trail connects with Boulder Creek. Hike 0.25 miles into the small amphitheater that holds the climb. | **Descent:** Alders exist at the top of the climb but bring a V-thread just in case.

2. Stairway to Stardom — WI3

50m
Harry Hunt & Stuart Parks, 2004

Climb moderate ice that may be partially or completely covered in snow, depending on conditions. The top (not pictured) is likely the crux. | **Approach:** Around 14 miles from the trailhead. This climb is easy to see from the river. Look for a steep canyon on the right with a mellow flow snaking up. | **Descent:** V-thread for rappel.

3. Superstition — WI4

360m
Harry Hunt solo, 1996

First climbed as a solo, this climb and the one next to it are excellent, fat flows of ice. When the sun hits the wall, it heats up and plenty of rocks may come cascading down. It is better to climb when cold or before the sun bakes the cliff. | **Approach:** 15.5 miles from the trailhead. These climbs are located up a drainage on the left side (west) of the river. Hike up the drainage to the climbs that are 150m off the river and 60m of WI2 will get you to the base of the climb. | **Descent:** V-threads for rappel.

4. Big Bubbler — WI3

240m
Harry Hunt & Dave Hart, 1996

An obvious flow of thick ice. The rockfall on this route is a serious hazard to be aware of. You can

(Courtesy Joe Connolly)

5. Boulder Creek Pillar Left   WI5

30m
Harry Hunt & Dave Hart, 1996

A classic freestanding pillar of ice that will give you everything you can ask for. This is why you came here. On one hand, these pillars may connect to form one continuous sheet leading to plenty of lines and lots of possibilities. On the other hand, they are often wet and may lead to a cold shower. | **Approach:** 20 miles from the trailhead. After about 18.5 miles the river splits in to a Y. Follow the left tributary and keep an eye out on the left (west) for the next flow coming from the hillside. Head up and gain approx. 200m of elevation before reaching the climbs. | **Descent:** V-thread for the rappel.

6. Boulder Creek Pillar Right   WI4+

30m
Harry Hunt & Dave Hart, 1996

This forms into an excellent line in its own right, as a free-standing pillar. The pillar may disappear when the face connects across, forming one large curtain of ice. | **Approach:** Follow approach information for *Boulder Creek Pillar Left*. | **Descent:** V-thread for the descent.

mitigate the dangers by climbing on the left side and not climbing while the sun is baking the cliff. You may still be exposed but the risk should be lower. The first two pitches are the most at-risk. An approach pitch of WI2 gets you ready for the climb. | **Approach:** Follow approach for *Superstition*. | **Descent:** V-thread for rappel.

(Courtesy Matthew Tucker)

Purinton Creek

(Courtesy Michael Meyers)

Distance: 3.5 miles

Approach: 90 minutes (ski)

Difficulty: WI5

ALERT: Avalanches can and will happen in this area. Know your surroundings and be aware of current conditions.

Access: Refer to page 139 for an overall map of the area. From Anchorage, drive the Glenn Highway north past Palmer, Sutton, and Chickaloon. The first parking option is a very small pullout at about mile 89.5, just before the Purinton Creek Bridge. Parking here is limited and very close to the highway. It's recommended, especially for those towing a snowmachine trailer, that you drive a bit further to the oversized pullout

located at mile 90.7. This large pullout is also the recommended parking spot when going to Boulder Creek. From the large pullout, take the well-defined snowmachine / ATV trail (online mapping refers to this trail as New Purinton Creek Trail) located at the western end of the pullout. Hiking or skiing this trail is possible; however, the terrain can be steep in sections so snowmachines are recommended. Keep to the trail as it goes straight north for a little over a mile then turns left and meanders through trees, marshes, and ponds. At about mile 2 of the trail, *Purinton Pillar* becomes visible two-thirds of the way down a ridgeline ravine to the north. Follow the main trail for another half mile, then break off and navigate to the base of this pillar. Unless another team has left a snowmachine trail to this route, you will likely have to put a trail in yourself.

Description: While there is only one route at this destination, it is worth it! A unique and secluded climb on the hillside, which sees a surprising amount of traffic.

1. Purinton Pillar   WI5

50m

Although this is the only route listed for this area, it is a worthy trip! This excellent climb can be a relatively quick approach compared to many of the other routes in this region. Of course that depends on conditions and equipment used. A large, often free-hanging pillar that pours into a rock amphitheater. The upper half of the climb is a pumpy vertical curtain. During good conditions, this climb may be heavily trafficked... and with good reason. | **Approach:** Follow directions listed on the previous page. | **Descent:** V-threads are needed to rappel.

Michael Meyers climbing high on the pillar with Steve Job on belay (Courtesy Michael Meyers)

Gravel Creek

(Courtesy Harry Hunt)

Distance: 6 miles

Approach: 60 minutes (snowmachine)

Difficulty: WI5+

ALERT: Avalanches can and will happen in this area. Know your surroundings and be aware of current conditions.

Access: For a rough location of the valley look at the Matanuska River Valley map on page 133. Recently, the word has been spreading about the climb up Gravel Creek drainage. Many never heed the calling because some consider it a long approach. But, in reality, this climb can be easily accessed in a day by ski. Pack your skis or snowmachine and head north on the Glenn Highway (from Anchorage) for just under 2 hours until you reach Victory Road (mile 94.6). Just west of the turnoff for Victory Road is a driveway on the south side of the road. Park near this driveway, say your prayers, and head down the road until you make your way onto the frozen Matanuska River. From here, directly across the massive river, you will find the opening into the Gravel Creek drainage. Depending on your mode of travel, the time to reach the pillar can be significantly varied.

Description: Although Gravel Creek may appear to have less bang for the buck in volume of climbs, do not let that dissuade you from the effort to reach the jewel. The approach to this route does take some effort, but it shows off a myriad of landscapes, including the sand towers shown in the picture above, to an undeniably beautiful piece of ice. Personal experience says you need to be savvy with timing to avoid rock bullets from above the route. Be careful not to disturb the neighbor's camp on the approach.

1. Gravel Creek Pillar   WI5+

55m

An easier line can be found on the right side of the climb, but as you move to climber's left, it gets harder. Expect many feet of vertical and very chandeliered ice before it slowly starts to ease off as you reach the top. If you want to get some more climbing in, you can continue for a couple more pitches of snow and WI3 ice. The surrounding cliffs can get dangerous when the sun hits them and they start to spit rocks. It is important to be aware of warming temperatures and to wear a helmet at all times. | **Approach:** This climb is located approximately 6 miles from the trailhead. | **Descent:** V-threads are needed to rappel.

Steve Wadleigh getting into the goods (Courtesy of Michael Meyers)

145

Glacier Creek

Author Chris Lindsey on Climb 3 (Courtesy Paul Guzenski)

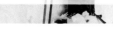

Distance: 12 miles

Approach: 1.5 hours (snowmachine)

Difficulty: WI4

ALERT: Avalanches can and will happen in this area. Know your surroundings and be aware of current conditions.

Access: Skirting across the front of the Matanuska Glacier and finding access into the mouth of the drainage seems somewhat direct, but this terrain is undulating and challenging. A more straightforward, albeit longer, approach is similar to that of Gravel Creek. Gain access onto the frozen Matanuska River and make your way upstream to the confluence with Glacier Creek. Access to the Matanuska River is easiest from either the Hicks Creek parking area or at the pullout near the Victory Bible Camp road via a road leading south to the river. Once on the Matanuska River, a trail will typically stay right as Glacier Creek turns south into the mountains. It may lift up off the river for a time before the trail makes its way back down to Glacier Creek proper. Several miles later, the crown jewel, *Threshold of a Dream*, will appear on your right. A mechanized approach is highly recommended in lieu of an arduous and lengthy ski.

Description: Wayne Mushrush described his attraction to ice climbing as one of aesthetics. A beautiful waterfall juxtaposed against an even more beautiful backdrop was all it would take to spark his interest to explore the backcountry. When Wayne talks of his first explorations into Glacier Creek with Martin Martinez in the late 1980s you could sense that this place was something special. The drainage takes you into the northern reaches of the Chugach Mountains, with impressive scenery. What Glacier Creek may lack in quantity of routes, it easily makes up with quality... and the overall backcountry experience.

N
S

Matanuska Glacier

The Last Frontier

Threshold of a Dream

Climb 3

Wayne Mushrush on the first ascent of The Last Frontier in 1990. (Courtesy Martin Martinez)

2. Threshold of a Dream WI4

55m
Martin Martinez & Wayne Mushrush, 1989

TOAD, as some call it, is the main prize in this valley. This route is typically in fat conditions because of the consistent water flow from above. The moisture that feeds this route comes out of what appears to be an avalanche-prone slope that must command your respect. This moving snow load from above can also change the length of this route by filling in the base as it slides. It is a classic water-ice route that everyone needs to check off their list. Climb thick hero ice (typically) up a consistent face. | **Approach:** Gaining access into the *TOAD* area on the west side of the Glacier Creek drainage takes some time and effort, as the start to these routes are several hundred feet in elevation gain and can take some time to reach. High snow load in the area is typical and skis and snowshoes should both be brought as tool options on the approach. | **Descent:** Rappel the route using alders and V-thread.

3. Climb 3 WI4

70m
Cash Joyce & Paul Turecki

It is unfortunate that this route never got a name when it was first climbed because it provides interesting terrain and is worth the effort. The route ascends a narrow gully that meanders up and right to the finish. It appears that it is likely a better climb in late season after freeze-thaw conditions help form some thickness. In 2018, a right curtain of ice extended to the base of the climb and thicker conditions prevailed throughout the full extent of the route. After climbing the first 20-30 feet of vertical terrain, the route makes its way through two more similar height curtains to the finish. | **Approach:** This approach is the same as *Threshold of a Dream*. Access the gully on the west side of the canyon floor using skis or snowshoes and move up steep terrain into this alcove; the route is on your left in a rock wall washout. | **Descent:** Rappel the route using alders and V-thread.

1. The Last Frontier WI4

25m
Martin Martinez & Wayne Mushrush, 1990

This route is known to include two pillars, but the first step of 25-30 meters is the main attraction. Climb a fat waterfall of consistent difficulty to reach a possible second step. | **Approach:** Last Frontier is the first main climb on the west side of Glacier Creek proper. It remains somewhat hidden because it is a few hundred yards off the canyon floor and located behind some rather tall pine trees. Access is straightforward and bush-whacking is likely. Snow shoes would make this approach less time consuming. | **Descent:** Rappelling the route is the easiest option to descend. But, neighboring terrain can make a walk-off possible.

(Courtesy Paul Guzenski)

Caribou Creek

Nathan Pooler on Robopick (Courtesy Michael Meyers)

Distance: 0.5 - 4.5 miles

Approach: 15 minutes - 2 hours

Difficulty: WI2 - WI5

Access: From Anchorage, drive the Glenn Highway north past Palmer, as the road meanders along the Matanuska River and between the Chugach Mountains and the Talkeetna Mountains. Just past the Matanuska Glacier, the highway makes a sharp left and dives down towards Caribou Creek. Drive over the bridge; on the northeast corner is where most find parking. If it's a low snow year, a large parking area to the left after the bridge may be accessible. The State of Alaska Department of Transportation is aware of Caribou's popularity and will typically try to keep at least a small pullout cleared of snow. If, however, the road shoulder or parking area isn't plowed, then it is highly recommended to NOT park on the shoulder of the highway and instead drive east up the hill and park in the pullout.

Description: Caribou Creek is located approximately 100 miles northwest of Anchorage and is probably one of the more popular ice climbing venues along the Glenn Highway. Pioneered in the late 1980s and early 1990s, this easily accessible drainage offers a number of routes varying in both height and difficulty. Some mixed routes on gear or bolts have also been put up over the years, but many aren't mentioned in this book. It usually freezes early and *Kid's Corner* is the first climb many will do at the beginning of ice season. Caribou Creek (most refer to it as Caribou) rarely shares the same climate as Anchorage or Palmer. Colder and dryer inland temperatures are common so don't skimp on a belay jacket. On the flip side, when it's warm, rainy and balmy

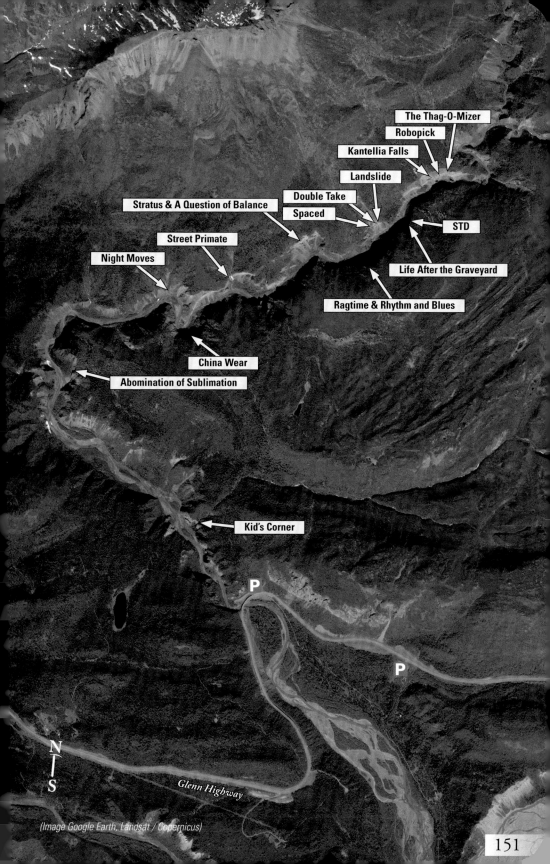

The Thag-O-Mizer

Robopick

Kantellia Falls

Landslide

Double Take

Spaced

Stratus & A Question of Balance

STD

Street Primate

Night Moves

Life After the Graveyard

Ragtime & Rhythm and Blues

China Wear

Abomination of Sublimation

Kid's Corner

P

P

N

S

Glenn Highway

(Image Google Earth, Landsat / Copernicus)

in Anchorage it's likely ideal ice climbing weather at Caribou. Although the drainage seems protected, it's a rare day when there isn't wind. Mid-December is typically when the creek is frozen enough to allow access beyond the first mile. Another option is a trail that begins at the parking area and leads to the top of *Kid's Corner,* or further. Hiking, snowshoeing, touring skis, skate skis, dog sled, and snowmachine have been used to access this area.

A climber starting the first pitch of Kid's Corner. This is an area classic and gets a surprising amount of traffic for being several hours away from Anchorage. It is usually done as a day climb, meaning about 3.5 to 4 hours of driving and around the same amount of time climbing for most parties. It's easy to see how adding an extra hour or two to the approach can make significantly long days when climbing in Caribou Creek. (Courtesy Michael Meyers)

1. Kid's Corner   WI3

180m
Scott Mignery & Chris Roach, 1990

This route earned its name after the FA members choose to neglect their fatherly duties in order to make the FA. This climb has become incredibly popular over the years for a number of reasons: it's very close to the road and access is rather straightforward; it forms in the early season when other routes haven't; it's deep within a cleft and protected from the often-brutal winds coming down Caribou; it's just a really enjoyable multi-pitch route for climbers of all levels.

Pitch 1: (WI3) The first pitch is about 15 meters of WI3 that is often aerated, chandeliered, or chopped out. The most trafficked pitch, don't be surprised if it somewhat resembles stairs by the latter part of the season. Above this pillar is a bolted anchor.

(Courtesy Michael Meyers)

1

Pitch 2: (WI2) From the bolted anchor, climb a short step of ice, then walk to the base of the second pitch, which is longer than the first but not as steep. It's usually wide at the bottom and narrows upward. If climbing this pitch in early season, don't be surprised by the presence of running water on or behind the ice. A large tree exists at the top of this pitch and is typically a good belay spot.

Pitch 3: (WI3) The third vertical pitch begins at the tree and, like the second pitch, is also wide at the base and narrows towards the top. Sometimes a small alcove exists near the top between the ice and the rock wall on the left.

Pitch 4: (WI2) The last of the route; a short section of WI2 takes you to the top.

| **Approach:** When approaching from the river, this climb is in a gully where you cannot see the start. Hike for 0.5 miles until you see a canyon on the right-hand side of the river, which is shielded by trees. There is usually a trail unless there's been a recent heavy snowfall. Follow the trail into the trees and it will lead to the base of the climb. You can also approach from the descent trail when the river is still flowing, following the descent information. | **Descent:** Alders or trees provide solid anchors on this climb. There are several options for the descent. Several anchors have been established on alders or trees in the gully, as well as bolted anchors. But, the easiest decent is a hike out from the top of the climb. After finishing the route, walk upstream 50-100 feet and look for the trail that leads off to the right. This trail will take you down the ridge towards the highway. Eventually, the trail meets up with what might be an old mining road that takes you down a gully and back to Caribou Creek bridge. Obviously, one must plan to carry everything up while climbing to take advantage of this exit. In early conditions, this trail provides access to the climb before the river is frozen.

2. Abomination of Sublimation   WI3

100m
Wayne Mushrush & Greg Golet, 1990

This route is characterized by its often yellow color; it looks like it is seeping through the hillside and pasted to the alders. The yellow look has led many to refer to it as Snot Wall.

Others just call it *Sublimation* for short. Windy conditions can exist here, so be prepared. There are many variations on the climb, although snow tends to stick to much of it due to the slabby nature and alder cover. The beginning tends to form in a steep vertical curtain that may add some difficulty. The first ascent was completed in -17 degree temperatures. | **Approach:** Approximately 1.5 miles upstream of the Caribou Creek Bridge, the creek does an S-bend and on the right is this route. This climb is located further down-river from *Kid's Corner* and is often easy to see, as it is close to the creek... but can be hidden partially from view during heavy snowfalls. Located on the right side of the canyon, walk through a short wooded section to the climb. | **Descent:** Many alders are available for setting up anchors.

3. Night Moves   WI2

50m
Wayne Mushrush, 1990

The first ascent was alone and during the night, hence the name. This low-angle route with short steps is typically in fat conditions, with cleaner ice towards the top and dirtier (yellow or brown) ice towards the bottom. A nice, easy climb that often forms up thick in wide steps. It is a tempting climb for anyone wanting to explore, but may not feel up to the difficulty that comes with the climbs further down-canyon. | **Approach:** 2.4 miles, located on the left side of the canyon just off the river after a split. A smaller channel will split right, stay left to reach this climb. | **Descent:** Trees and alders exist on top, but be ready for a V-thread if you need to do two rappels.

4. China Wear   WI4

30m
Scott Mignery & Chris Roach, 1990

China Wear is on the right side after the second bend. A tempting treat after hiking for so long through the canyon. This is an enjoyable climb, with the final curtain being steeper than it often looks. The surrounding cliffs seem to shed a lot of rock, be careful at the base. Winds can be brutal at this location. At the creekside, begin up low angle snow/ice to the vertical wall; build an anchor on top of the curtain. | **Approach:** Approximately 2.5 miles up-creek from the Caribou Creek Bridge, located on the right side of the canyon. This climb remains hidden until you round a large bend. You will pass *Night Moves* and then continue to the next sharp bend. The climb will be easily visible on the right and starts off the river. | **Descent:** There used to be alders at the top of this climb, but they seem to have fallen down. There is a tree at the top, but it is too far beyond the lip to be very useful. Be prepared to build a V-thread.

5. Street Primate   WI2

20m
Wayne Mushrush & Greg Golet, 1990

This climb can be seen from the old miners' shack and is located on the other side of the river (left). The top is normally in fat conditions and is a fairly wide curtain. The climb on the right is called *Polar Shrimp (WI1)*, a relatively easy solo. | **Approach:** 3 miles from the trailhead. Located on the left side of the river, across from the miners' shack. Hike up some snow and through alders to reach the base of the route. | **Descent:** Alders exist on top for rappel.

6. Stratus   WI4-

25m
Wayne Mushrush & Greg Golet, 1990

Stratus is one of two climbs located 400ft above the river in a small alcove. This is the lower left of the two climbs and ends in a rock face. The bottom 15m tend to be steep, with the rest being more laid back. Another first ascent that was done at 10 degrees Fahrenheit, which is common for Caribou, as it tends to hold the cold. | **Approach:**

(Courtesy Michael Meyers)

3.4 miles up the creek from the Caribou Creek Bridge is a rock alcove on the left side, just as the creek makes a 90-degree turn to the right. Hike up the slope to a short section of vertical ice that is less steep above. | **Descent:** Bring V-thread or extra slings for a bollard.

7. A Question of Balance   WI4+

45m
Wayne Mushrush & Martin Martinez, 1990

Climb a 20m pillar, followed by low-angle ice to an ice formation under an overhanging roof. The first ascent party said, "it shook like a rubber band". | **Approach:** 3.4 miles up the creek from Caribou Creek Bridge is a rock alcove on the left side, just as the creek makes a 90-degree turn to the right. Hike up the slope to *Stratus* then right for 50 meters to the route start. | **Descent:** Rappel via rock gear or V-thread.

8. Ragtime   WI4

85m

The right of two climbs that originate from the same portion of canyon rim. This climb doesn't form often and, most years, it may be nearly non-existent, with just a few small pillars on route. Start on a steep curtain and climb through steps to another steep pitch before the canyon rim. | **Approach:** Same as *Rhythm and Blues*. | **Descent:** Alders exist on the canyon rim and on route, but a V-thread is recommended as backup.

9. Rhythm and Blues   WI4

85m
Wayne Mushrush & Sean Baginski, 1990

This is the left of two climbs and the more consistently forming of the pair. Climb a narrow runnel of ice followed by another short and vertical step to a small amphitheater above. Another 15-20m of ice exists at the back of the amphitheater. | **Approach:** Mile 3.5 from Caribou Creek Bridge; located on the right side of the canyon just around the bend from *Stratus* and *A Question of Balance*. Starts just off the river. | **Descent:** There are alders, but it is best to bring a V-thread for additional rappels.

(Courtesy Josh Pickle)

10. Spaced   WI2/3

40m
Chris Roach & Scott Mignery, 1990

The FA party named this route after one of them forgot their ice tool at the top of *Double Take* and they had to climb *Spaced* to retrieve it. In the mid-2000s it was changed when a landslide in the area significantly impacted the area. Hike approximately a 60m to the base of this route, then climb moderate angle ice to the top.
| **Approach:** Mile 3.8 from Caribou Creek Bridge; the left of three climbs located on the left side of the canyon. A short hike over rock and snow will put you at the base of the route.
| **Descent:** Rappel via vegetation or V-thread.

11. Double Take   WI5

50m
Chris Roach & Scott Mignery, 1990

A steep and wonderful climb that was originally rated WI5. Surprisingly, it retained the difficulty even after a landslide in the mid-2000s changed it and *Spaced*. The landslide blocked the river and managed to form a new line to the right of *Double Take*, expanding this area. A rock band above allows this route to form a 15m vertical ice curtain followed by a short step above.

It's not often that landslides and large natural disasters work in our favor when it comes to ice and rock climbing. In mid-2000's it created another large flow for more ice goodness, but it also highlights the dangers of nature.

Depending on conditions, very low angle ice may continue for a good distance upward. As the area above settles from the landslide, these climbs may change in size. | **Approach:** Mile 3.8 from Caribou Creek Bridge; the middle of three climbs located on the left side of the canyon. From the creek, hike the slope for approximately 30m to the base of the route. | **Descent:** Previous tree anchors were wiped out by the landslide. Vegetation exists, but a V-thread is helpful.

12. Landslide   WI3

60m

This climb didn't exist before the mid-2000s landslide. It is located to the right of *Double Take*. Just after the landslide, it dwarfed the other climbs in the area creating a wide sheet of ice and robbing *Double Take* of surprisingly little. As time goes on, this climb will likely change in appearance. A wide swath of ice that flows over mellow steps. | **Approach:** Same as *Double Take*. | **Descent:** There is vegetation on the route but as the area changes it could reduce the amount. Be prepared for a V-thread.

157

(Courtesy Michael Meyers)

The picture above shows *Life After The Graveyard* with the largest flow that has been reported. It usually forms thin and significantly smaller. During such large flow years, this climb may be as easy as WI3. These routes are a good example of the ever-changing nature of ice climbing. For years they didn't form, only to come back steady and consistent.

13. Life After the Graveyard   WI3

30m

An interesting climb that sometimes forms to the right of *STD*. It never used to form, but in recent years, has been coming in; though this climb is still fickle. The year the guidebook was written, it created a wide sheet that appears to be expanding — life after death indeed. The picture above shows the climb in somewhat unrealistic conditions. When it forms, there is often a curtain of thin ice that leads up to a ledge with alders. | **Approach:** Same as *STD*. | **Descent:** Vegetation exists on the ledges.

14. STD   WI4-

30m
Joel Schihl & Ian Thomas, 2001

STD and *Life After the Graveyard* are rarely forming climbs that appear to be more consistent in recent years than they were in the past. *STD* forms more often and into a larger climb than its neighbor. Climb a flow of ice about body-width wide as it heads up to a ledge below a rock face. Occasionally, this climb will have a second pitch that comes down from the canyon rim and requires a pull over the roof to access. This ups the difficulty and length, but it forms even less often than the rest of the climb. Scramble just off the river to the base of the route. | **Approach:** Mile 4.0 from Caribou Creek Bridge; located on the right side of the canyon just after the *Double Take Area* around the bend. | **Descent:** There are alders at multiple levels of the climb to use for rappel.

(Courtesy Josh Pickle)

15. Kantellia Falls   WI5

120m
Scott Mignery & Chris Roach, 1990

Named after the FA party's attempt to keep this route secret:

"What have you been climbing?"
"Can't tell ya"

Climb a nearly vertical 15m ice curtain to a large step above. The step is often a good spot to bring up your belayer. Moderate low-angle ice continues for another 30 meters. A short 5m ice curtain will put you in the alder brush at the top. | **Approach:** Mile 4.2 from Caribou Creek Bridge. From the creek, hike approximately 25m to the base of the ice. | **Descent:** Rappel via vegetation and V-thread.

↑
⑮

(Courtesy Sherrie Soltis)

(Courtesy Josh Pickle)

16. Robopick	**WI5**	**17. The Thag-O-Mizer**	**WI4**

90m
Scott Mignery & Chris Roach, 1990

Climb several steps of WI3 for approximately 40m to the base of the ice curtain. It's recommended you bring up your belayer here. Climb the nearly vertical curtain for approximately 50m or until there is no more ice; this is the crux pitch. | **Approach:** Mile 4.3 from the Caribou Creek Bridge and next to *Kantellia* *Falls.* | **Descent:** Be prepared to place a V-thread anchor to descend off this route. No natural protection is available.

100m
Steve Davis, Feb. 1996

The Thag-O-Mizer is just past *Robopick* and is the last climb on the left before Caribou Creek waterfalls on itself. Climb a low-angle flow to the base of a 10m near-vertical curtain. Continue to the right and up low-angle and stepped ice to anchor trees at the top. | **Approach:** Mile 4.4 from the Caribou Creek Bridge. | **Descent:** A single 70m rappel will get you to the base of the curtain. Alders and V-thread for the descent.

The Matanuska Glacier in the Matanuska River Valley is a great summertime ice climbing destination. With easy access and a short approach the glacier sees plenty of climbing and is even host to the Mountaineering Club of Alaska's yearly ice climbing festival

Briana Brendle climbing her way out of a moulin on Matansuka Glacier during the MCA's Ice Festival (Courtesy Chris Walden)

SEWARD

Surrounded by high mountain peaks and located at the head of Resurrection Bay, Seward is about a 2.5-hour drive south from Anchorage on the Seward Highway. During the summer months the small community bustles with tourism — largely due to the numerous cruise ships passing through. Seward is also the home of the famous Mount Marathon race, which is considered by many to be the toughest 5k running race in the world. During the winter, the community is a bit more slow-paced, as skiing, snowmachining, and climbing in the surrounding mountains becomes the focus. Winter weather in Seward itself can vary drastically from rain to negative temps, so make sure you plan your climbing in the area accordingly.

Rebecca Mamrol on Climb 3 in Victor Creek (Courtesy Chris Walden)

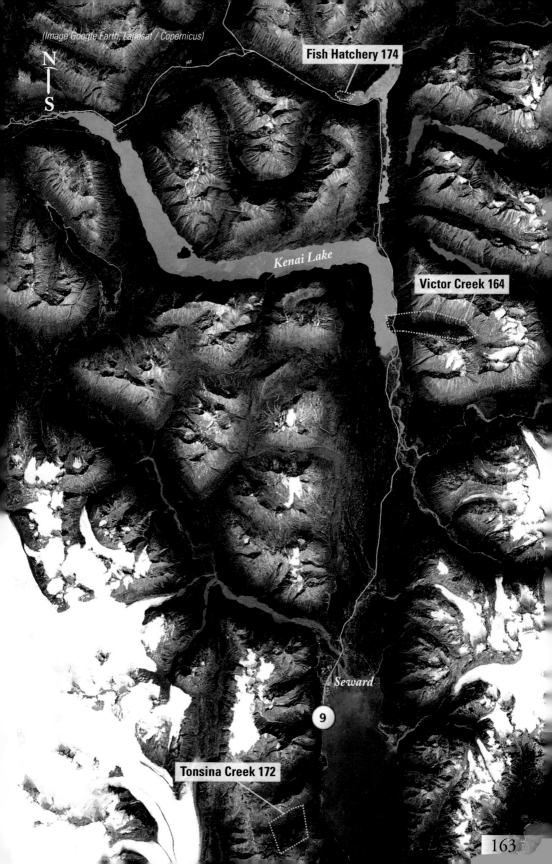

(Image Google Earth, Landsat / Copernicus)

N
S

Fish Hatchery 174

Kenai Lake

Victor Creek 164

Seward

9

Tonsina Creek 172

163

(Courtesy Ben Fisher)

Victor Creek

10

Distance: 0.5 - 1.6 miles

Approach: 10 minutes - 2 hours

Difficulty: WI2+ - WI5+

ALERT: Avalanches can and will happen in this area. Know your surroundings and be aware of current conditions.

Access: From Seward, drive about 20 miles north on the Seward Highway and then park in the small pullout located near the southeast corner of the Victor Creek Bridge. If coming from Anchorage, drive the Seward Highway south for approximately 2 hours and park in the same pullout. From the pullout, you can access the base of the routes by hiking up the creek for approximately 20 minutes;

however, the creek isn't always frozen, so bring waders if you want to stay dry. Another option is to cross the highway bridge and then hike the established Victor Creek Trail for approximately 45 minutes to the top of the canyon. From the top of the canyon, it isn't always easy to see where the routes start forming, so plan on peeking over the edge every now and then. It is also worth noting that the canyon depth can be deceiving, so be prepared to do multiple rappels depending on the length of your rope(s). The Victor Creek Trail continues beyond the canyon and might be the better option if you are trying to reach the climbs further up the valley, such as *Victor Valley 1, 2, and 3*.

Description: Not easily noticeable, Victor Creek flows out of a deep canyon on the mountainside of the Seward Highway. Multiple routes of varying difficulty are a short hike from the highway. There are many smaller flows in the canyon that are not located in this guide.

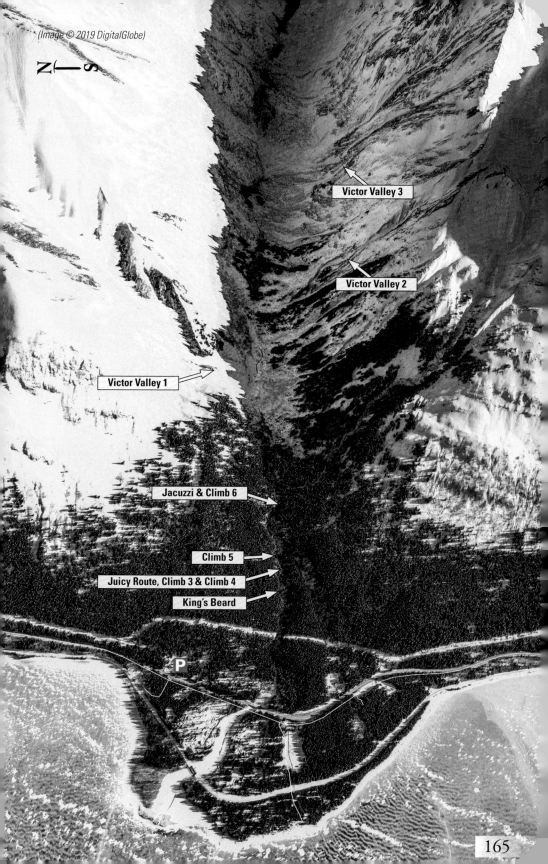

(Image © 2019 DigitalGlobe)

Victor Valley 3

Victor Valley 2

Victor Valley 1

Jacuzzi & Climb 6

Climb 5

Juicy Route, Climb 3 & Climb 4

King's Beard

P

165

(Courtesy Michael Meyers)

1. King's Beard   WI5+

70m
Eugene Beutler & Cash Joyce, 1999

The pride of Victor Creek, this route is only a 10-15 minute hike from the highway. An open creek at the very base of the route is common and may require some technique to get around. Once that is negotiated, begin by climbing a low-angle ramp of thin ice to a small alcove above on the right. This route is known to drip even in the coldest of conditions, and it is at this alcove that you and the rope might start getting wet (really wet). From the alcove, climb left up a short section of moderate-angled ice to the main flow. From here up, and depending on conditions, the route may be a super-fat vertical pillar or an overhanging and chandeliered curtain. Whatever you encounter, count on it to be in your face and pumpy. This route sun rots from the top down, so don't be surprised to find soft ice at the very top. | **Approach:** Follow the creek upstream and within a few minutes you'll be hiking past ice flows on your left (north side of the canyon). Just past these flows, the canyon narrows significantly and it is here where open water is most common. The depth of the creek here is not unsafe, however, it can be higher than a pair of rubber boots, so come prepared. *King's Beard* is located just past this narrow section. | **Descent:** Large trees at the canyon rim allow for an easy rappel to the base.

2. Juicy Route   WI4

85m
Cash Joyce & Bjorn Olson, 1999

Start by climbing up a wide section of WI4 for approximately 30m. Depending on conditions and time of year, this section can be thin — keep that in mind when it comes to your ice screw selection. Above this, the ice thickens and becomes less steep for the remaining 35m. There is an additional 20-30m of WI2 past the anchor. | **Approach:** Similar to *King's Beard*, an open creek at the very base of the route may need to be navigated. | **Descent:** Anchor trees exist, though a V-thread may be necessary, as many of the trees along the side of the route are dead or dying. Rappel to the canyon bottom and don't forget to keep your rope ends out of the water below.

(Courtesy Michael Meyers)

Dax Walden and Caden Hall on Climb 5. A great climb for new and beginning climbers. (Courtesy Chris Walden)

3. Climb 3   WI3

50m
Cash Joyce

Just to the right of *Juicy Route*, start by climbing WI3 for approximately 20m, then begin making your way left and up another 20-30m of lesser-angled ice to the vegetation anchor. | **Approach:** Same as *Juicy Route*. | **Descent:** The anchor tree typically has a lot of small branches that may make it difficult when trying to put webbing around the trunk.

4. Climb 4   WI3/4

50m
Cash Joyce

Located just past *Climb 3*, this route begins by climbing 5m of either vertical or moderate-angled ice (your choice) to a very long section of WI2 ice and snow above. From the bottom, it may appear as if the route goes all the way to the canyon rim, but it doesn't. | **Approach:** Located just past *Climb 3* on the same side of the river. | **Descent:** Vegetation for making an anchor is plentiful; however, much of it is dead so be prepared to make a V-thread.

5. Climb 5   WI2+

60-100m
Cash Joyce

This route is tucked away on the north side of the canyon and can easily be missed if you're hiking with your head down. Depending on conditions, start by climbing a 20m section of 45-degree ice. From here on up, the ice steepens to no more than WI2+. An ice screw anchor is necessary if belaying from above the 45-degree section. | **Approach:** Located approximately 50 meters upstream of *Climb 4*. | **Descent:** There is plenty of vegetation at the top and along the route to rappel from, but not all is alive so be prepared to make a V-thread.

6. Climb 6   WI3

30m
Cash Joyce

This relatively short route is just downstream of *Jacuzzi* on the south side of the canyon. An open creek at the base is common and it may require the leader to cross a frozen bridge downstream and then traverse/climb back to the main flow. At the main flow, begin on a slightly vertical curtain for 10 meters. Above that, the difficulty lessens to WI2 for another 15-20m. | **Approach:** Continue upstream past *Climb 5* and you will see this route and *Jacuzzi*, which form above an open pool. | **Descent:** Devil's club can get thick towards the top of this route so be prepared to V-thread if you want to avoid getting pricked.

7. Jacuzzi WI3

30m
Eugene Beutler & Bjorn Olson, 1999

Located at the very back of the canyon, this route is formed by Victor Creek water-falling into the canyon from the valley above. The base of the route is guarded by a large splash pool with the appearance of water in a jacuzzi. It is also a reference to one member of the FA team falling backward into this pool while trying to gain access to the bottom of the route. The most difficult aspect is accessing the ice. Start by traversing the rock wall on the left-hand side. Once on the route, you should be able to gauge the quality of the ice and whether it is worth moving higher. Keep in mind there is a large amount of water behind this ice and if you fall through, or the route collapses, it may be difficult to get out if you are roped. It's likely you'll be able to hook all the way to the top. The top of the route is the start of the canyon. | **Approach:** Continue upstream and this route is at the back of the canyon 10-20 minutes from *King's Beard*. | **Descent:** Bring V-thread material.

8. Victor Valley 1 WI4

50-70m

ALERT: This climb is within a large avalanche zone. As such, make sure you are familiar with your surroundings and know the conditions. Formed by a small drainage of meltwater within a large avalanche runout zone, this route may not be present or visible from below if the area is blanketed by deep snow. Start by climbing low-angle snow and ice for about 20 meters followed by a shorter section of slightly steeper ice. A 15-20m near-vertical pillar leads to snow or frozen ground above. | **Approach:** This route is located on the north side of the valley, just beyond the canyon. As such, it's recommended to hike the well-established Victor Creek Trail, which begins near the northeast corner of the Seward Highway bridge over Victor Creek. Hike the trail as it meanders through the forest on the north side of the canyon. The trail is usually well-traveled and, due to the dense forest, it is typically free of deep snow, which makes for easier and faster hiking. After approximately 1 mile, the forest abruptly ends at a large clearing that is also an avalanche

169

runout zone. Being mindful of avalanche conditions, turn left and hike up for about 20-30 minutes to the base of this route. | **Descent:** Vegetation at the top is limited and rappelling via V-thread is not recommended. Walking off the top of the route is possible.

9. Victor Valley 2 WI3

250m

The climb is located on the north side of Sheep Mountain, higher in elevation than the more popular climbs down in Victor Creek. So when the lower creek climbs have melted out, these deliver the goods earlier and longer in the season. Depending on conditions, pitch 1 can be a rope-stretcher at 70m. The ice is fat and wide and can accommodate multiple parties. At the top of the first pitch, the ice chokes down onto a narrow ledge and, in good conditions, the belay can be set here. Be aware the ice on pitch 1 can still be wide and fat; however, later season warmer temperatures can leave the top-out void of ice with areas of smooth slate, possibly snow

covered. If these conditions exist, continue up to a small alder or break out the pitons. Continue up the canyon mixing in steepish snow and easy ice climbing for approximately 2 rope lengths. This can be pitched out or makes for easy solo climbing. Pitch 2 is 30m of thick WI-fun that lands you on a great ledge to belay. Continue up to a 8m top-out and enjoy the amazing views of Kenai Lake and Andy Simons Mountain.

| **Approach:** The approach can change depending on the time of the season. *Early Season:* Take the Victor Creek Trail back 2.1 miles where the trail drops down near the river into a bed of cottonwood trees. Cross the river and head up the steep drainage that snakes up climber's left approximately 800 feet to the start of the climb. Beware: the valley walls in this drainage are steep and in avalanche run-off terrain. *Late Season:* Take the Victor Creek Trail back approximately 2.7 miles and cross where a large boulder chockstone forms a bridge across the canyon or avalanche debris has formed snow bridges over the canyon. Trend up and climber's right through two groves of trees to a bench above the snaking drainage

(Courtesy Chris Walden)

listed in the Early Season approach. This location is a few hundred feet directly below the climb. | **Descent:** Vegetation is sparse so you'll need to rappel the route via V-thread.

10. Victor Valley 3   WI3

180m

This route consists of three distinct pitches of smooth, non-undulating ice. The first two pitches are the steepest and may be rope-stretchers if using 60m ropes. The top pitch is lesser-angled, but worth climbing just to say you got to the top. | **Approach:** Depending on conditions, getting to this route can be an all-day adventure, which is why an alpine start is recommended. Begin at the Seward Highway and hike the established Victor Creek Trail through the forest to the valley beyond. Avalanche terrain abounds in the valley, so it's a good idea to put on (or turn on)

any avalanche gear before leaving the forest. It is here in the clearing that this north-facing route is visible on the south wall of the valley, about halfway up from the valley floor. Now that you are away from the trees and past the canyon, hike, ski or snowshoe back to the creek and begin to follow it upstream. Within a short distance, the creek flows through yet another canyon that is much smaller than the one downstream. After negotiating your way through or around this canyon, you'll want to start trending right and making your way up to this route. Don't be surprised if during the approach you see numerous other ice flows on both sides of the valley. Many are not mentioned in this book; however, all are considered to have already been climbed | **Descent:** Vegetation is sparse, so you'll need to rappel the route via V-thread.

The upper valley is a great place to explore during low avalanche potential.

Tonsina Creek

Distance: 3 miles

Approach: 1.5 - 2 hours

Difficulty: WI5

ALERT: Avalanches can and will happen in this area. Know your surroundings and be aware of current conditions.

Access: From the SeaLife Center in the City of Seward drive south on Railway Avenue / Lowell Point Road to the community of Lowell Point. From there, continue south on the same road, which changes to Tonsina Creek Road, to the parking lot for the Lowell Point State Park Recreation Area. Hike south on the Caines Head / Tonsina Creek Trail, hiking approximately 1.5 miles. After crossing the hiking bridge over Tonsina Creek turn right and follow the creek upstream to your destination. Note that this area is prone to avalanches, so be mindful of current conditions. Secondly, this area is prone to flooding, which means access may change.

Description: Providing beautiful scenery no matter the season, Tonsina Creek flows east out of the mountains into Resurrection Bay just south of Seward. Depending on conditions, one may find numerous ice formations in this area, but *Cathedral Falls* is the real prize.

1. Cathedral Falls	WI5

80m

A large volume of water flowing over a rock ledge creates this stunning route. Depending on recent temperatures, this route may be thin in some places and thick in others. When the authors first attempted this route, it had numerous overhanging mushrooms on ascent-left while ascent-right and center was smooth and visibly thin. Long ropes are recommended, but even then it may require a belay just short of the top. Another pillar exists immediately above. | **Approach:** From the Caines Head / Tonsina Creek Trail, turn right and begin hiking up the creek. Approximately 1 mile from the trail, the drainage separates into a Y. You'll want to stay left and continue hiking up the creek for just under a mile until just past the large alcove on your left. Turn around and the route is at the back of the alcove. | **Descent:** V-thread for the descent.

(Courtesy Michael Meyers)

Fish Hatchery

(Courtesy Chris Walden)

Distance: 0.5 miles

Approach: 30 minutes

Difficulty: WI4

Access: From the City of Seward, take the Seward Highway north for approximately 32 miles. The fish hatchery complex is located on the north side of the highway and just after Trail Lake. If coming from Anchorage, the drive south on the Seward Highway takes approximately 1.5 hours.

Description: The hatchery, which has been active since the early 1980s, is a great destination in the summer for fish viewing. Little goes on in this area during the winter... until the sun comes out to light up the rock faces, which are also host to a few bolted mixed routes.

1. Fish Hatchery   WI4

80m

This route forms in somewhat of a cleft and is easily visible if you know where to look. Begin on a short series of steps, followed by a vertical section that ends at the tree above. From there, climb the moderate ice to the top. | **Approach:** Park in the pullout, which is typically plowed, then hike the trail around the lake to the rock face on the opposite side. You can also hike across the lake if it is well frozen. | **Descent:** Plenty of vegetation for rappel.

(Courtesy Chris Walden)

The unique formations of Hung Jury, Valdez (Courtesy Michael Meyers)

VALDEZ

Located in the northeast corner of Prince William Sound, the small community of Valdez is equally known for its extreme heli-skiing terrain as it is for being the terminus of the Trans-Alaska Pipeline. However, before all that the mid-to-late 1970s frozen multi-pitch waterfalls within easy driving distance of the community became the focus of world-class climbers. In 1976, the late Jeff Lowe with John Weiland completed the first ascent of *Keystone Greensteps*. Within the next 10 years, the local climbing community, largely fostered by the late Dr. Andrew Embick, exploded with a number of new pioneered ice routes. The first Valdez Ice Climbing Festival was held in 1983 and, by 1986, the climbing scene had just under 200 first ascents. In 1989, the late Dr. Embick published *Blue Ice & Black Gold*, a comprehensive guide to all pioneered ice routes to-date. Since then, a number of additional first ascents have occurred and Valdez still remains a popular destination for those wanting to test themselves on worldclass, multi-pitch ice routes.

(Courtesy Zachary Sheldon)

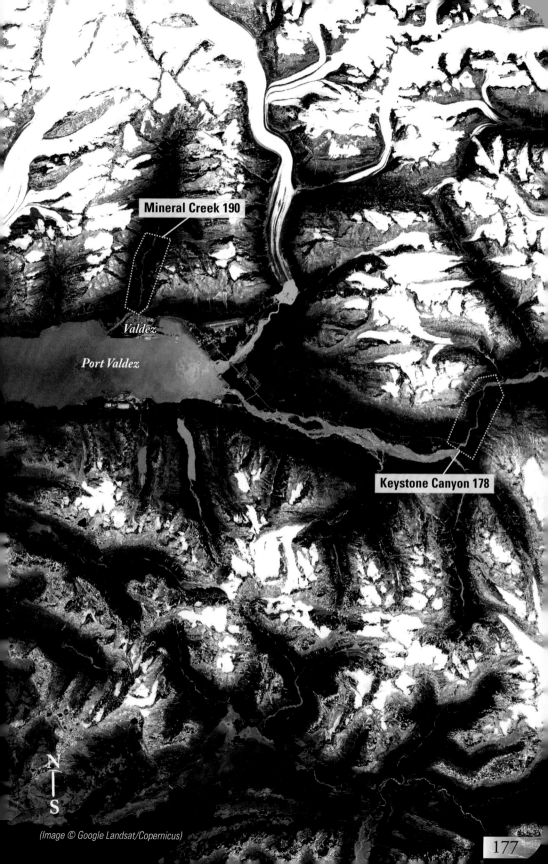

Mineral Creek 190

Valdez

Port Valdez

Keystone Canyon 178

N
S

(Image © Google Landsat/Copernicus)

(Courtesy Zachary Sheldon)

Keystone Canyon

Distance: 0.15 miles

Approach: 0 - 15 minutes

Difficulty: WI2 - WI6-

ALERT: Avalanches are common in Valdez and some of the areas cross avalanche paths for the approach or descent.

Access: From Valdez, follow the Richardson Highway out of town towards Anchorage for around 17 miles. The canyon will be obvious and if you don't see any ice, then you're there in the summer and should buy the rock climbing book. If you're coming from Anchorage, you'll have to pass through the canyon to get to Valdez. Just keep an eye out for the giant pieces of ice lining the canyon.

Description: Keystone Canyon is one of the more stunning ice climbing areas in this book. It has a storied history with ascents by legendary climber Jeff Lowe and local crushers, such as Brian Teale, Carl Tobin, Roman Dial, Chuck Comstock, and the list goes on. If you haven't made a trip to the canyon yet, it is time to pack your bags and head out. The previous guidebook for the area, *Blue Ice and Black Gold* by Andrew Embick, M.D. included hundreds of climbs throughout Valdez and is still a great resource for the areas not listed here, if you manage to find a copy. Hopefully, those climbs will make it into future editions of this guidebook. Another highlight of Valdez ice climbing throughout the years has been the festival that brings climbers from around the world to this small town. It is one of the oldest climbing festivals in the country, dating back to 1983. It was resurrected recently from a short hiatus and continues to lure climbers each year to this wonderful destination.

Hanging Tree Right & Left

Cidersicle & Popsicle Pillar

The Bight

P.O.S

Flying Cloud

Bridalveil Falls

Simple Twist of Fate

Glass Onion

Keystone Greensteps

Love's Way

Horsetail Falls

Hung Jury

Fang Gully

Mudslide

N
S

(Image © USGS The National Map: Orthoimagery)

179

1. Hanging Tree Right   WI4

35m

Jim Jennings & Carl Tobin, Dec. 1977

The right pillar tends to be shorter and less steep than its direct neighbor. Continue left in a gully after the pillar to reach the top of *Hanging Tree Left* to descend. | **Approach:** Mile 15.4. There are two parking possibilities. The recommended option is to park on the right side of the road before the guardrail, just prior to the double bridge over the Lowe River. There is a large wooden sign stating the history of the highway tunnel at this parking area. The other option is to park on the side of the road just across from the climbs. The Department of Transportation does not recommend parking on the road. | **Descent:** There are alders above that can be used to lower, or you can continue up the gully and hike out to the right, down Snowslide Gulch. Be aware of avalanche conditions before descending this way.

Hanging Tree Right and Left will usually require some amount of river crossing to get to the base, although an ice bridge does occasionally form. When you're heading to the ice, make sure to keep an eye out for the many mixed lines that exist in Keystone Canyon. There are some great mixed lines to the left of this area, which may have bolts or require rock gear placements.

(Courtesy Zachary Sheldon)

2. Hanging Tree Left   WI4

35m
Andrew Embick, Dana Hollister & Carl Tobin, Mar. 1980

The left of two close climbs in this small area. It forms steeper and taller than *Hanging Tree Right*. You can finish at the top of the ice when it reaches the gully by moving left or continuing in the gully to the top. | **Approach:** Same as *Hanging Tree Right*. | **Descent:** There are alders above that can be used to lower, or you can continue up the gully and hike out to the right down Snowslide Gulch.

3. Cidersicle   WI3

12m
Paul Henstridge solo, Feb. 1987

The short pillar to the left of *Popsicle Pillar*. This route generally does not form as a solid flow from top to bottom, but is often protectable on screws in the spring due to the ice blobs that allow for placements. Steep and unique thin ice climbing. | **Approach:** Mile 15.4. Park on the right side of the road before the guardrail, just prior to the double bridge over the Lowe River. There is a large wooden sign stating the history of the highway tunnel at this parking area. From the sign, hike 100m upstream following a washed out trail that used to lead to the tunnel entrance. Turn right at a small depression that is often marked with flagging material; head straight up this slight drainage to the base of *Popsicle Pillar*. The first 3/4 of this approach trail is shared with *The Bight*. | **Descent:** Rappel off a large pine tree on either side of the climb.

4. Popsicle Pillar   WI2

25m
Andrew Embick & Rick Parks, Dec. 1979

Popsicle Pillar is a fun and sometimes surprisingly challenging route up a medium-sized pillar that forms into a fat flow. The left side is vertical and challenging with great stemming and hooks. The right side is generally less than vertical and easier than the left. | **Approach:** Same as *Cidersicle*. | **Descent:** Rappel off a large pine tree.

5. The Bight   WI3

35m
Mark Bloomfield & Art Mannix, Feb. 1980

Forms as a two-tiered climb consisting of vertical ice separated by a small section of moderately steep and sometimes snow-crusted ice in the middle; the upper section consists of a steep crux that will keep you fighting all the way to the top. | **Approach:** Mile 15.4. Park on the right side of the road before the guardrail just prior to the double bridge over the Lowe River. There is a large wooden sign stating the history of the highway tunnel at this parking area. From the sign, hike 100m upstream following a washed-out trail that used to lead to the tunnel entrance. Turn right at a small depression that is often marked with flagging material, head direct toward *Popsicle Pillar*, but turn right 30m before those climbs and hike under the small cliff face. Follow the gully to the base of *The Bight*. | **Descent:** Rappel from large trees at the top.

Michael Meyers and Matt Tucker, stoked to be climbing in Valdez during the Valdez Ice Fest. (Courtesy Chris Walden)

6. P.O.S	**WI3**

25m
D. Mullet & Rich Parks, Mar. 1978

A consistently fat piece of ice on the left (west) side of the canyon, just off the highway when approaching from Valdez. The right forms vertical and pumpy while being the most consistent. The left is more moderate, but has a higher flow rate behind the ice, causing it to be more of a shell over the rock. There are three solid stainless steel bolt anchors on the left side of the cliff above, which can be used to toprope the left side of the ice, as well as several mixed routes. It is possible to access the anchor from the wagon road above. | **Approach:** Mile 13.9. Parking is on the left side of the road in a large, long parking lot across from *Bridalveil Falls*. Hike up the road 200m to the climb. | **Descent:** Primary descent is from the large pine tree at the top of the cliff. It may require a few meters of easy mixed climbing to reach the tree.

7. Flying Cloud	**WI5+**

110m
Andy Embick & Bill Lorch, Feb. 1981

The large feature that forms just left of *Bridalveil Falls,* often connecting at the base. The top half generally forms fat, while the lower half consists of pillars and technical chandeliered ice that clings to the vertical canyon wall. When in, this technical climb is an amazingly memorable experience. The first ascent of this route was intended to be a public demonstration of ice climbing during the Valdez Winter Carnival. It turned into an 8-hour ascent that finished long after the crowds had gone home, highlighting that while ice climbing is a great sport, it can be less than thrilling to spectate. | **Approach:** Mile 13.9. Park in the large parking lot on the left side of the road and hike across the road directly to the base of the route. Crossing the river may be necessary. | **Descent:** Alders exist on top, but a V-thread is recommended for additional rappels.

8. Bridalveil Falls   WI5

230m
Jim Jennings, Clif Moore & Carl Tobin, Dec. 1977

This climb is usually broken into four pitches, with an additional WI3 pitch available 100m beyond the top of the canyon rim.

Pitch 1: (WI4+) Steep, fat and beautiful ice climbing for 30m up the vertical face will get you to an easier ramp. Follow the ramp to just below the vertical curtains and set up the belay here, or off to the left side by the cave. There is a fixed anchor inside of the cave that is used primarily for rappel. This large hidden cave forms against the rock face behind pitch one and is a stunningly beautiful sight.

Pitch 2: (WI4+) Start on the steep curtain that covers the cave, for a second crux to reach a long section of moderate WI3+ climbing. This leads you to the base of the Killer Piller. Belay from either side of the pillar.

Pitch 3: (WI5) The Killer Pillar crux. Some consider it the crux of *Bridalveil Falls* or *Keystone Greensteps*. Climb 20m of steep ice for the final hard crux to a long ramp of WI2. Belay on the left side off V-threads and screws.

Pitch 4: (WI3) Continue scrambling low-angle ice before reaching tiers of WI3 that bring you to the canyon rim. There is a pine tree on top for an anchor.

| **Approach:** Mile 13.9. Park in the large parking lot on the left side of the road and hike across the road directly to the base of the route. Crossing the river may be necessary. | **Descent: Pitch 4 : (50m)** From the top of the rim on the right hand side, rappel from a large pine tree that often has tat to an ice blob on the left-hand-side before the Killer Pillar. **Pitch 3: (50m)** Alders or V-threads to the ledge at the base of the Killer Pillar. **Pitch 2: (60m)** V-thread or alders on climber's left of the route. This rappel should put you into the cave on a 2-bolt anchor. **Pitch 1: (60m)** Rappel from a 2-bolt anchor inside the cave. A walk-off is also possible from the top of pitch 4. Hike right across the canyon rim for 1/4 miles and descend the snow slide gully to the right of *Love's Way*. This descent is made easier later in the year as avalanches and heavy snow cover bury ice that forms in the gully.

9. Simple Twist of Fate   WI5-

75m
Carl Tobin & Rick Parks, Dec. 1979

Simple Twist starts on the top of the same approach ramp as *Glass Onion* and *Hooligan* on the left-hand-side of the ledge. This route forms a shotgun barrel for the belayer. Finding a good belay area to protect the belayer is an important factor in climbing this route and will greatly amplify the enjoyability of this line. The grade tends to remain consistent throughout the entirety of the route, as it forms a clean line without a lot of tiers. The second half of the climb splits in two, with each taking a similar difficulty. | **Approach:** Mile 13.9. Park in the large parking lot on the left side of the road and hike across the highway and the Lowe River. Scramble the wide snow field below *Glass Onion*; the left side of the approach will often consist of some easy WI2 scrambling to reach the large ramp below *Glass Onion*. | **Descent:** Rappel from V-threads and alders. A final rappel off alders is possible from the top of the approach pitch.

10. Glass Onion   WI5-

120m
Carl Tobin & Roman Dial, Jan. 1981

From the left side of the ramp, climb 5-10m of *Simple Twist of Fate* before traversing right to a series of ledges with little ice; use alders for protection to reach a ledge before the climb proper. Trend right up ledges as the ice gets continuously thicker, until you get to the top of the canyon rim. This route is in reference to the John Lennon song of the same name. | **Approach:** Mile 13.9. Park in the large parking lot on the left side of the road and hike across the highway and the Lowe River. Scramble the wide snow field below this route; the left side of the approach will often consist of some easy WI2 scrambling to reach the large ramp below *Glass Onion*. | **Descent:** Alders on top will get you to the lowest section of good ice that will take a V-thread, or back to the start ledge which has some alders. A long helicopter rappel should get you back to the large ramp. Check that your rope ends touch before rappelling. A walk-off is also possible and is the same as *Bridalveil Falls*.

11. Hooligan   WI2

25m
Bob Pudwill & Dave Berg, Mar. 1980

A thin, low-to-medium quality route that ascends directly under *Glass Onion* and ends at the ramp. This should never be climbed with anyone above. Scramble to the alders and build an anchor above and right of the route. Watch for falling ice above, as *Glass Onion* sheds its skin. | **Approach:** Mile 13.9. Park in the large parking lot on the left side of the road and hike across the highway to the Lowe River. Scramble the wide snow field below *Glass Onion*, heading directly to the base of the route. | **Descent:** Rappel from alders.

(Courtesy Jordan Haffener)

12. Fooligan WI2

12m
Roman Dial solo, Apr. 1985

A short pitch that generally isn't worth heading to on its own. Flows from the steep roof below *Glass Onion*. | **Approach:** Same approach as *Simple Twist of Fat*e. From the large ramp that forms at

This area of Keystone Canyon is the most popular, as it includes a high concentration of classics easily visible from the road with a short approach. It is also the primary venue for the Valdez Ice Climbing Festival.

the top of *Hooligan* head right to the base of this climb. Hug the back of the ledge along the cliff to avoid debris from above. | **Descent:** Rappel from alders.

13. Keystone Greensteps   WI5

200m
Jeff Lowe & John Weiland, Jan. 1976

An ultra-classic of Valdez and a roadside Alaskan testpiece. Most parties should leave a full day to climb and descend this route. Normally climbed in four pitches.

Pitch 1: (WI5) Start up the left side of the wide flow at the base and stay left for 55-60m of climbing to the top of the first tier. Move left to alders on a snow ledge or build a V-thread anchor in the center of the ice.

Pitch 2: (WI5) Climb straight up a full pitch of steep ice and anchor on the left using alders or on the right side in a hidden cave using a V-thread or screws. Don't forget to explore the cave.

Pitch 3: (WI5) Start up the steep columns before reaching a series of ledges. V-thread on the ledges for an anchor.

Pitch 4: (WI4+) Straight up the left side to the top of the canyon rim. There is plenty of vegetation for anchors, but the best is at the base of a small rock face on the right, beyond the canyon rim. Pitch 3 and 4 can be linked for one long pitch.

| **Approach:** Mile 13.9. Park on the south end of the large parking lot on the left side of the road and hike across the road directly to the base of the route. Crossing the river may be necessary. | **Descent: Pitch 4 & 3: (70m)** Rappel from alders at the top of the canyon rim. Pitch 3 and 4 can linked with 70m ropes or can be broken up with a V-thread in the middle. Rappel to the ledge and use a V-thread for the next pitch. **Pitch 2: (60m)** Rappel to the ledge on the left-hand-side that has alders for the anchor. From the top of pitch 2, it is possible to walk-off left using the ledge system below *Glass Onion*. **Pitch 1: (60m)** From the alders, rappel back to the ground. These rappels are all long rope stretchers. Always tie knots in the end of your ropes.

14. Love's Way   WI6-

110m
Andrew Embick & Carl Tobin, Mar. 1980

Climbing high to the upper walls of Keystone Canyon is the elusive and often sought after *Love's Way*. When touching down, this route consists

of overhanging daggers, candlestick pillars and chandeliered curtains. | **Approach:** Mile 13.9. Park on the south end of the large parking lot on the left side of the road and hike across the road directly to the base of the route (up a steep snow slope). | **Descent:** Rappel the route using alders and V-threads.

15. Horsetail Falls   WI3

80m
John Weiland solo, Dec. 1975

A broad fan of ice that forms just off the road. This is a high volume flow that always has water ripping beneath the ice. The feature often forms and crumbles numerous times throughout a season. A spectacular climbing experience when in good conditions, usually after a good cold snap. Bolted anchors now exist on this climb. It is taller than it looks. | **Approach:** Mile 13.4. Park on the left side of the road in a large parking lot at the base of this photogenic roadside attraction. | **Descent:** There is a 2-bolt anchor 50m up on the left side of the flow, and a second anchor 50m further on past the technical climbing.

16. Hung Jury   WI4

55m
Steve Clautice & Carl Tobin, Feb. 1978

An iconic formation of large bells created by the unique winds that whip around the corner through the canyon, which sculpt this amazing climb. Thread your way up the bulbous formations, often tiptoeing on delicate ice. | **Approach:** Mile 13.4. Park on the left side of the road in a large parking lot at the base of *Horsetail Falls*. Hike 300m toward Valdez, then step over the guardrail and cross the Lowe River, heading directly to the base of the route. | **Descent:** Rappel from alders on the upper left corner of the route. Use great caution on the descent to avoid dislodging any cicles on the free-hanging bulbs. The descent is something not to be trifled with.

17. Fang Gully   WI2

90m
Jim Jennings, Bill Kitson & Jim Meigs, Nov. 1977

Consists of two enjoyable moderate pitches in a

(Courtesy Michael Meyers)

(Courtesy Michael Meyers)

gully to the right of *Hung Jury*. Hike delicately over parts of the ice where water might pool under the surface. Be prepared to use several ice screws as directionals to ensure the rope stays dry. | **Approach:** Same approach as *Hung Jury*, but hooks right at the base to a gully. | **Descent:** Rappel the route. Vegetation on top, but V-threads are necessary for additional rappels.

18. Mudslide   WI3

90m
Rick Parks & Andrew Embick, Dec. 1979

From the top of the scree and snow, follow the left-trending gully up moderate ice that is often thin and rarely connects from top to bottom. Usually broken into two pitches with the first ending where the ice turns left and the second pitch being the crux. | **Approach:** This thin formation is on the left side of the canyon when approaching from Valdez. From the parking lot of *Horsetail Falls* at mile 13.4, hike 400m toward Valdez then turn right and scramble up the scree directly to the base of *Mudslide*. | **Descent:** Rappel the route using alders on top and V-threads for the second rappel.

Rebecca Lewis, Nathan Kutcher, Hayden
Carpenter and Nick Weicht on Wowie Zowie
(Courtesy Thomas Tapp)

189

Hayden Carpenter on Wowie Zowie (Courtesy Thomas Tapp)

Mineral Creek

Distance: 2.2 miles

Approach: 1.5 hour (hike)

Difficulty: WI2+ - WI6+

ALERT: High avalanche threat exists throughout the bulk of Mineral Creek Canyon. Be aware of conditions before heading out.

Access: Mineral Creek Trailhead is located off Mineral Creek Road at the North end of Valdez. Follow Mineral Creek Trail for 1/4 miles and cross the metal bridge that is milemarker 0 for these climbs. Continue after the bridge for 2 miles and these climbs are on the right-hand-side of the valley across the river. Crossing Mineral Creek may be challenging, but ice bridges generally exist. Breaking trail

to the climb will add time to the approach. Mineral Creek is open to motorized access along the mining road, which goes up canyon far beyond the climbs listed in this book, and can significantly save on approach time. If approaching by snowmachine, stay off of all designated cross-country ski trails or risk a fine and jeopardizing future access to the area. Free snowshoes are available for rent at Prince William Sound College in Valdez.

Description:

This seven-mile-long valley is flanked on both sides by 7000-foot peaks that offer stunning views along with fantastic opportunities for ice climbing, skiing and exploring. While most of the routes near town have been climbed decades ago, there are still an absurd amount of new routes to be explored beyond the stamp mill (five miles up the valley). The creek flows from Mineral Creek Glacier and other tributaries located north of Valdez. These drainages are home to hundreds of climbs, both explored and awaiting discovery.

Cool Runnings

Climb 2

Climb 3

Chillout Syndrome

Wowie Zowie

Dr. Weiland's Evil Eye - Pillar of Light

Robe River Dr

Hanagita St

Eklutna St

Dadina St

Copper Dr

Lowe St

Chena St

Cottonwood Dr

Jago St

Alatna St

Valdez

W Klutina St

Fairbanks Dr

W Pioneer Dr

Galena Dr

Egan Ave

Clifton Ct

Meals Ave

Egan Dr

N

S

4

(Courtesy Zachary Sheldon)

1. Cool Runnings   WI3

300m

Climb the narrow ice gully located several large flows beyond *Wowie Zowie*. Start the route down low on easy-angle ice / snow that leads into a small amphitheater, where the interesting climbing starts. A 30m wide and 30m tall amphitheater that holds a prize pitch of moderate ice in the gully. Continue following along this ribbon of ice up the enjoyable mini-canyon for two consistent pitches of thick blue flow. An excellent beginner alpine adventure. | **Approach:** 2.3 miles from the steel bridge at the entrance of Mineral Creek Canyon. Head straight to the base of the climb from the trail. | **Descent:** Rappel the route. V-thread material is necessary; some alders exist.

2. Climb 2   WI4

250m

Start by climbing the left side of a wide flow of ice for a great 50m pitch of WI3. Followed by another pitch of low-angle ice and moderate snow that will lead you to the base of the featured attraction. This climb is the left of the two large flows above, and is one of the finest pieces of WI4 to be found in the Valdez area. It has consistently fat and stellar conditions, offering unique exposure and a great panoramic view of the inspiring Chugach mountain range. After the crux pitch, another 100m of mellow WI3 will get you to the top. | **Approach:** 2.2 miles from the steel bridge at the entrance of Mineral Creek Canyon. Head straight to the base of the climb from the trail. Located in the drainage immediately left of *Wowie Zowie*. | **Descent:** Rappel the route on V-threads and alders.

3. Climb 3   WI4

300m

Climb the left side of a wide flow for a great 50m pitch of WI3. This is the right side of two large flows. Scramble the snow field up and right to the base of another great flow of spectacular blue ice. This crux pitch can be climbed from either the right (WI4) or left (WI5+) depending on desired difficulty. After the crux, continue moderate ice until the flow eventually ends in the snowfields

high on the mountainside. This route and the one before are excellent alpine experiences with only moderate commitment and difficulty. | **Approach:** Same as *Climb 2*. | **Descent:** Rappel the route on V-threads and alders.

4. Chillout Syndrome   WI2+

40m

This route makes for a fun warm-up or a moderate opportunity if you're looking for a low commitment and user-friendly climb. | **Approach:** 2.2 miles from the steel bridge at the entrance of Mineral Creek Canyon. Head straight to the base of the climb from the trail. | **Descent:** Alders exist on top of the climb for rappel.

5. Wowie Zowie   WI6

120m
Andrew Embick & Carl Tobin, 1981

Probably the proudest line in the Valdez area. This true testpiece clings proudly to the sheer rock walls of Mineral Creek Canyon. Usually climbed in two or three distinct pitches, this unique monster requires skilled route finding through a forest of pillars and daggers. Several anchors can be found behind the featured flow that offer protection from debris. It is best climbed in the morning to early afternoon, as it begins to get sun and can start to shed. This route is also exposed to avalanche hazard, so be aware of conditions. High in objective hazards with temperature swings, avalanches, poor placements and everything else you can think of. | **Approach:** 2.1 miles from the steel bridge at the entrance of Mineral Creek Canyon. | **Descent:** Alders for the top rappel and V-thread for the second. A possible walk-off to the left exists — scramble down a ramp and make one rappel.

6. Dr. Weiland's Evil Eye   WI6+

150m
Carl Tobin & Nora Tobin, Dec. 1996

Climb a pillar that is 30m to the right of *Wowie Zowie* to a snowy ramp. Continue following the left runnel of ice through extremely steep and varied terrain. This ribbon occasionally goes as an ice climb during good spring conditions, but often requires mixed climbing and rock protection. Finishes on the large curtain of overhanging ice. One of the most difficult routes in the Valdez area, even upping the game from *Wowie Zowie*. First attempted by John Wieland and Jim Sweeney, but they aborted when Weiland took a 60 foot fall into clean air and emerged unscathed. | **Approach:** 2.1 miles from the steel bridge at the entrance of Mineral Creek Canyon. Head straight to the base of the climb from the trail. | **Descent:** Alders for rappel.

7. Silver Haired Daddy   WI5+

120m
Brian Teale & Rodrigo Mujuica, Dec. 1996

Depending on conditions, the upper pitch of this route can be reached by scrambling up a 45-degree ramp to the snowy ledge beneath the upper pillar or by first climbing the pillar that is the start of *Dr. Weiland's Evil Eye* and traversing right. The second pitch is a full pitch of gloriously steep and consistent pillar climbing. End where

the flow trickles out of the rock face using screws or a V-thread for the anchor. | **Approach:** 2.1 miles from the steel bridge at the entrance of Mineral Creek Canyon. Head straight to the base of the climb from the trail. | **Descent:** Rappel the route. V-thread material is necessary.

8. Pillar of Light   WI6

130m
Brian Teale & Chuck Comstock, Dec. 1996

The first pitch is the same start as *Silver Haired Daddy*, but continues traversing right until under a thin line of delicate pillars and daggercicles. It is not as consistently forming as its left neighbor and is much more sustained. Follow the thin flow of cicles for an exciting full 60m pitch. | **Approach:** Same as *Silver Haired Daddy*. | **Descent:** Rappel from alders at the top and V-threads for additional rappels.

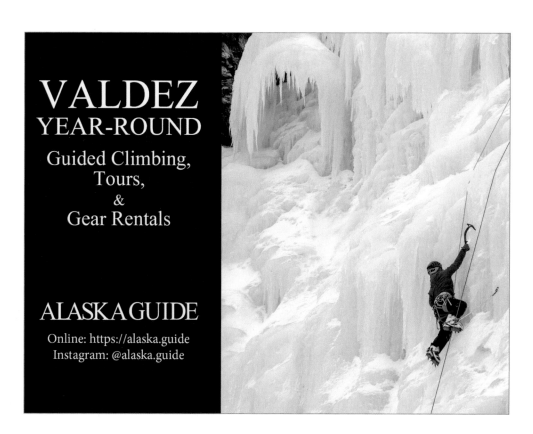

NABESNA

This area sits in one of the more beautiful spots of the state, at the foothills of Wrangell - St. Elias National Park. Nabesna is far from nearly everything, with little to no development nearby. Amenities are few in this sparsely populated area, so you'll want to bring your own supplies and be fairly self sufficient. This isolation provides a unique opportunity to experience the true backcountry of Alaska. Low temperatures can be extreme in the dead of winter, which is why most climbers choose to visit in early-and-late ice season. In more recent years, snowfall levels have dropped dramatically, which has made an approach by foot somewhat of a necessity. Given the somewhat lengthy approach times, climbing in Nabesna may result in big days on big routes.

Katherine Delia and Rachel Newell on the approach (Courtesy Andrew Holman)

(Image © 2019 DigitalGlobe/NASA)

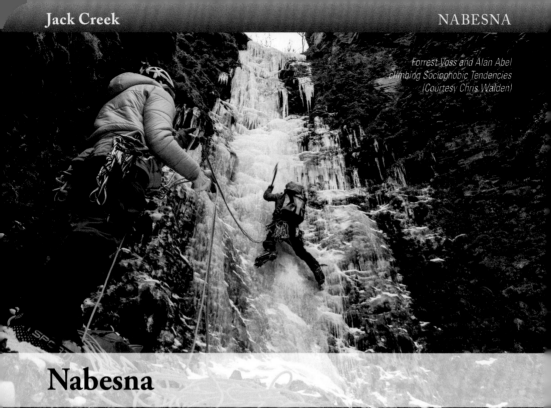

Forrest Voss and Alan Abel
climbing Sociophobic Tendencies
(Courtesy Chris Walden)

Nabesna

JACK CREEK

Distance: 1.25 miles

Approach: 60 minutes

Difficulty: WI4 - WI5

ALERT: Avalanches can and will happen in this area. Know your surroundings and be aware of conditions.

Access: From Anchorage, drive the Glenn Highway north approximately 3 hours to Glennallen, then turn left (north) on the Richardson Highway and drive approximately 15 minutes to the Tok Cutoff. Take a right and follow the Tok Cutoff for approximately 1 hour to the Slana - Nebesna turnoff. Take a right at the turnoff and follow the road to your destination. You'll want to overnight in the area so it's recommended to make

reservations at one of the local lodges. Park your vehicle on the shoulder of the road at approximately mile 35 of the Nebesna Road. Depending on conditions, hike, ski or snowshoe east through trees and across uneven tundra for just over a mile to a main canyon on the south flank of the mountain that holds the obvious *Sociophobic Tendencies* and *Spring Fling* routes. The terrain at the base of the mountain can be very cobbly, so watch your step as you hike another 45 minutes or more to the routes above. Approach and descent may consume a good portion of the day, which is why an early morning start is recommended.

Description: This remote area provides the bulk of the climbs in Nabesna. There are a variety of choices, all within view on the west side of the river, that can deliver differing features, difficulty, and commitment. Climbs like *Spring Fling* will take you through alpine terrain with a near-mountain summit finish, in an isolated environment. The canyon to the south of *Sociophobic Tendencies* is lined with options, like the testpiece *Wing and a Prayer* or the meandering *Corridor*.

1. Sociophobic Tendencies   WI4

350m

Sociophobic Tendencies is similar but slightly more challenging than its big brother next door, *Spring Fling*. A fun ice line in good conditions but in thinner conditions be prepared for some mixed climbing, as ice may not form on all the benches. The first pitch is 15m of WI3. The next few pitches wander through a narrowing slot canyon that offer exciting views and fun WI2-3. Follow 100m of moderate terrain and short 3m vertical pillars to a beautiful WI4 pillar. Bring a standard alpine ice rack (screws, a set of nuts, small selection of iron, single small range of cams). | **Approach:** The same as *Spring Fling*. This climb is located in a gully to the left of *Spring Fling*. | **Descent:** Rappel down the steep ice and down-climb the easy sections — an alternate descent is to traverse towards *Spring Fling* and hike off (using the beta for the *Spring Fling* walk-off). While a walk-off may be tempting, the rappel is likely the best descent.

2. Spring Fling   WI4

350m
Kristian Sieling, Jeff Young & Harry Hunt, Apr. 1997

Start by climbing a 25m pillar to low-angle terrain, followed by several short ice steps that end at a large boulder. Depending on conditions, there could be short sections of mixed climbing to negotiate near the boulder. Moderate terrain above leads to another steep pillar. Several hundred meters of moderate climbing lands you at the top of the route. | **Approach:** *Spring Fling* is located within the first prominent gully and should be visible from the road, depending on conditions. | **Descent:** This route can be difficult to descend. It is possible to rappel the route using V-threads. As an alternative, one can hike off the peak after ascending the route. After leaving the ice at the top of the route, stay left up through loose talus for 30m. Traverse right under the large rock outcrop and hike your way down a long boulder field. Stay left out of the drainage to avoid a steep drop-off on the right during descent. Expect the walk-off to take over an hour.

(Courtesy Chris Walden)

(Courtesy Chris Walden)

3. Wing and a Prayer   WI5

50m
Harry Hunt & Danny Kost, Mar. 1996

Wing and a Prayer is typically a large ice flow that forms over several steps. It is found near the back of the gully on the right. Climb a short section of low-grade water ice to a nearly vertical curtain above. Above the curtain is another step of slightly less steep ice.
| **Approach:** *Wing and a Prayer* and *The Corridor* are found in the gully to the left of *Spring Fling.* Instead of hiking to the base of *Spring Fling,* head around the mountainside into a wide gully on the far left. This will lead to a small canyon where *Wing and a Prayer* is on the right-hand side. | **Descent:** Rappel the route. V-thread is necessary.

(Courtesy Michael Meyers)

Forrest Voss on the third pitch of Sociophobic Tendencies (Courtesy Chris Walden)

(Courtesy Andrew Holman)

4. The Corridor   WI4

650m
Dave Lucey & Harry Hunt, Mar. 1998

The Corridor is located at the very back of the canyon and just past *Wing and a Prayer*. As the canyon narrows towards the rear, this route forms. The route can be an all-day adventure, as it provides multiple short ice pillars separated by hiking sections. It ends at a large bowl near the summit. A great route for practicing alpine climbing. | **Approach:** *The Corridor* and *Wing and a Prayer* are found in the gully to the left of *Spring Fling*. Instead of hiking to the base of *Spring Fling,* head around the mountainside in a wide gully to the far left. This will lead into a small canyon where *Wing and a Prayer* is on the right-hand side and *The Corridor* is at the back of the canyon. | **Descent:** Rappel the route. V-thread is necessary.

PARKS & DENALI HIGHWAYS

About 210 miles north of Anchorage, or 150 miles south of Fairbanks, and situated at the intersection of the Parks Highway and Denali Highway, is a sparsely populated community of Cantwell. 20 miles north of Canwell is the entrance to Denali National Park. The chance to see Alaska wildlife, massive glaciers and North America's tallest peak brings tourists by the thousands through this area during the summer months. Come winter, however, the average temperature plummets into the negative digits, making it ideal for dog mushing and snowmachining. Fairbanks climbers have been coming to the nearby ice routes for years, whereas the climbers from Anchorage and Mat-Su areas have plenty of nearby ice to keep them busy through the dark winter days and typically don't make the journey here until late winter / early spring.

A summertime view of the Denali
Highway (Courtesy Chris Walden)

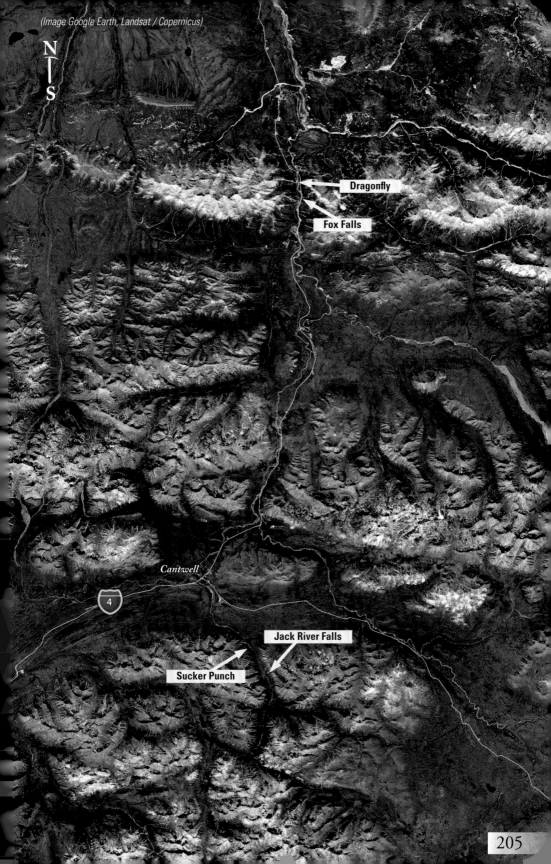

(Image Google Earth, Landsat / Copernicus)

N
S

Dragonfly

Fox Falls

Cantwell

4

Jack River Falls

Sucker Punch

205

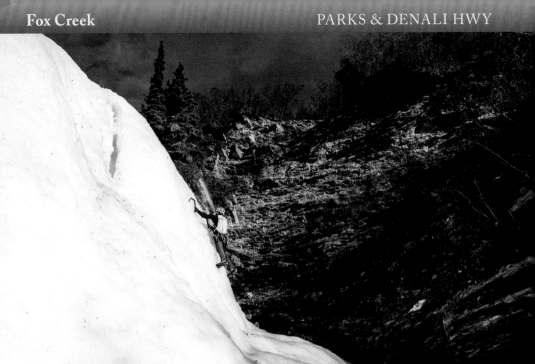

Parks Highway

Chris Walden on a late season ascent of Fox Creek (Courtesy Chris Walden)

FOX CREEK

Distance: 0.1 miles

Approach: 10 minutes

Difficulty: WI3

Access: Drive north from Anchorage on the Parks Highway. This will lead toward Eagle River and Wasilla. Continue through Wasilla and head north toward the Denali Highway. This drive will take most parties around four hours one-way, quite the day's expedition. Stay on the Parks Highway until mile 241.2, where there is parking for Fox Creek.
Description: The George Parks Highway runs from downtown Anchorage to Fairbanks (after 360 miles). From Anchorage to Wasilla, it is known as the Glenn Highway, but then splits and continues as the Parks Highway past Wasilla. Along this road you'll see a plethora of wildlife and beautiful sights. Unlike the Glenn Highway, after it splits toward Palmer, much of the driving tends to follow low, wide valleys until it heads through the Alaska Range. Here, the mountains get closer to the road. There are other climbs along this great stretch of road that will hopefully make it into the next edition, but for now, these few climbs give a great starting point for the area.

1. Fox Falls   WI3

35m

When in fat, this location is perfect for multiple parties looking to hone their lead skills. For those trying to get lots of climbing in a limited time, climbing this route as well as others nearby will surely take up all your Alaskan daylight. It is possible to toprope this route by gaining access through the gully on the left and setting up the anchor on a tree. | **Approach:** From the road,

follow the Fox Creek drainage upstream until you arrive at the climb. Beward of Fiasco Notch a small ice step that has caused broken bones.
| **Descent:** A tree with a big chain for the anchor.

DRAGONFLY CREEK

Distance: 0.1 miles

Approach: 10 minutes

Difficulty: WI3

Access: Drive north from Anchorage on the Parks Highway. This will lead toward Eagle River and Wasilla. Continue through Wasilla and head north toward Healy and Fairbanks. This drive will take most parties around four hours one-way making it a long days expedition. Stay on the Parks Highway until mile 242.2, where there is parking for Dragonfly Creek in a large lot on the left-hand-side of the road before the bridge. When accessing from Fairbanks, drive south on the Parks Highway and continue past Healy. The parking lot will be on the right-hand-side after crossing Dragonfly Creek. This takes about 2 hours and is easily done as a day trip.
Description: Commonly a day adventure when driving south from Fairbanks, this route can be paired with *Fox Falls* to create an enjoyable day out on moderate ice.

2. Dragonfly	WI3+

50m

This route is comprised of several steps that can be climbed in one pitch to make a decent line. The first step is comprised of some interesting ice that leads up to a second, more moderate step. Perhaps the best reason to visit this climb is for the view of Nenana Valley below. | **Approach:** It is actually located downstream from the bridge; depending on conditions, you may need to rappel from the top of the route to reach the base.
| **Descent:** Walkdown trails descend on both sides of the climb, large trees for rapping and a bolted anchor station exist at the top of the climb.

207

Denali Highway

A view into the Jack River drainage (Courtesy Chris Walden)

JACK RIVER

Distance: 4.5 - 5.5 miles

Approach: 1.5 hour (Ski)

Difficulty: WI3/4

ALERT: Avalanches can and will happen in this area. Know your surroundings and be aware of current conditions.

Access: From Anchorage, drive Glenn Highway north to Cantwell on the Parks Highway. From Fairbanks, drive the Parks Highway south to Cantwell. At Cantwell, take the Denali Highway east approximately 3.8 miles and park at the end of the plowed section, usually after Golden North runway and Drashner Lake. The Denali Highway is closed during winter months from this point. The trail is usually well-trafficked leading south from the parking lot and can be as quick as 15 minutes on a snowmachine. Once on the plateau overlooking Jack River head due east toward *Jack River Falls*, which is located on the left side of the valley.

Description: Due to the driving distance, climbing *Jack River Falls* from Anchorage or Fairbanks is best done late season (mid-March to late-April) and over a couple days so as to allow time to visit other nearby routes. Waiting too late in the season may give time for the river to open back up, making access more difficult. Cantwell motels often have reduced nightly rates during winter months that make staying for the weekend doable.

1. Sucker Punch   WI3
180m

The first pitch is around 30m of wide, relaxing WI3 that narrows into a steep canyon at the top; setup the belay here. Either unrope and solo up a few pitches of easy terrain, or continue on approximately 100m where the canyon walls constrict into the last pitch of alpine fun; 38m of total ice climbing. The final section ramps up 8m of narrow, steepening ice. North facing and stays in condition longer due to its aspect and higher elevation. | **Approach:** Follow the approach to the plateau perch overlooking Jack River valley. From this highpoint, the climb is visible looking south across the river. Follow the trail down to the valley floor and find a good location to cross Jack River. Head up the drainage as it snakes up the mountain to the first pitch of ice. | **Descent:** V-threads for the descent.

2. Jack River Falls   WI3/4

150m

This south-facing route forms in a large drainage coming down from the ridgeline on the east side of the valley. The first 30-40m of the route is mostly a hike on crampons and requires very little ice tool placement. The second pitch, which can be a real rope stretcher, climbs up and over several large and nearly vertical benches. Even with 70m ropes, proper ice screw placements are crucial if wanting to climb all the benches in a single push. Above the second pitch, the ice disappears into snow. Follow the drainage up a few hundred meters to another short pitch of WI3/4 ice, which is often a reddish-yellow color. | **Approach:** Follow area approach. | **Descent:** Descend the route by V-threading the steep portions and hiking or downclimbing the non-technical sections.

(Courtesy Chris Walden)

A climber high on Bridalveil Falls with the belayer hidden in the cave. Flying Cloud looks thick and technical on the left (Courtesy Chris Walden)

Matt Tucker leads a thin Sea Wolf in Homer. Bottoming out screws in this type of situation may just fill them up with silt from the bluff (Courtesy Chris Walden)

HOMER

The City of Homer rests at the end of the Sterling Highway on the picturesque northern shores of Kachemak Bay. Homer is a popular tourist destination during the warmer months, due largely to its reputation as the halibut fishing capital of the world. More than just fishing however, the city is also well-known for its artsy culture and the distinctive Homer Spit, a long gravel bar that extends into Kachemak Bay. Not to be overlooked during the winter months, Homer has a small ski area, groomed cross-country ski trails; and the Caribou Hills to the north provide exceptional terrain for snowmachining.

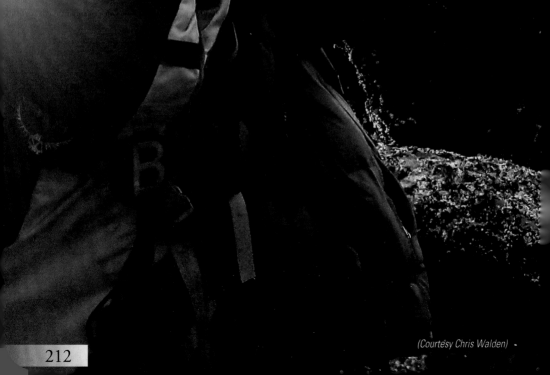

(Courtesy Chris Walden)

Sea Wolf

Boredwalk

Redline

Dog Day

Mt Augustine Dr

1

Hunter St

P

Close to Home

Granola Cruncher

Saltwater Dr

N
S

(Image © 2019 DigitalGlobe)

Homer Bluffs

(Courtesy Chris Walden)

Distance: 0.6 miles

Approach: 15 minutes

Difficulty: WI3 - WI5

ALERT: Do not get caught in the tide. Make sure you are aware of the current tides in the Homer area, as water levels rise to the base of the ice on a few routes.

Access: Drive the Sterling Highway out of Homer and when going up the big hill, make a left turn onto Saltwater Drive. Park at the very end of the road then walk about halfway back to the highway, turn right and walk through the alders to the edge of bluff. A pair of 60m ropes will allow a rappel past the steep section of the bluffs. On the rappel, the route to the left is *Close to Home*. Once on the beach (looking towards the water) walk right for the larger and more difficult routes or walk left for the easier climbs.

Description: Multiple routes offering various difficulties, beautiful scenery and the sound of ocean waves are just a few of the many reasons why this area is not to be missed when conditions are right. The downside, however, is that these routes have been forming less often over the last 10+ years. To make it even more challenging, when they do form, they will sometimes melt out in a matter of hours, so watch the weather and time your trip appropriately. It's a good idea to keep track of the tides in this area, as they do come all the way up to the base of the routes; it's recommended to not leave personal belongings on the beach when climbing. The Homer Bluff, similar to bluffs along Turnagain Arm, largely consists of easily erodible soils. As such, routes may vary from year to year. There can be a lot of ice in this area, however for this book we only included the more prominent routes. Lastly, environments near salt water can be extremely harsh on your metals and ropes. Following any climbing in this area, a thorough wash of your gear is recommended.

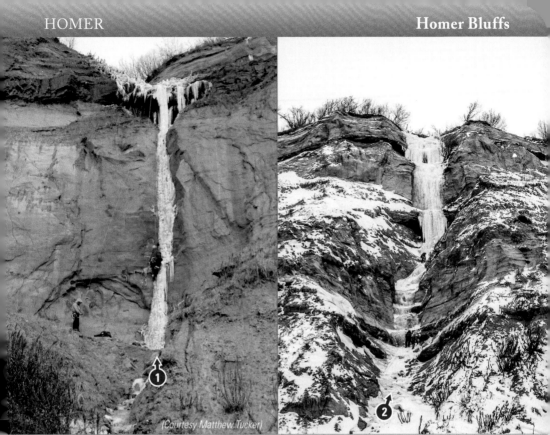

(Courtesy Matthew Tucker)

Robert Suenram and Travis Mcalpine climbing Sea Wolf.

1. Sea Wolf   WI4+

70m
Jim Sweeney & Billy Day, 1989

This climb is just left of *Boredwalk* and around
a small bend. It starts with a thin, steep pillar
and leads into a gully. The pillar is usually not
very wide and constitutes a real challenge for
protection. A classic for the area. | **Approach:**
Just past *Boredwalk* and around a small bend
about 0.55 miles from *Close to Home*, it is one of
the last climbs on the bluff. | **Descent:** There are
alders on the top of the bluff but this route will
likely require a V-thread for additional rappels.
Rock gear or pins may also be necessary during
lean years.

(Courtesy Chris Walden)

2. Boredwalk   WI4

70m
Billy Day, Steve Garvey & Jim Sweeney, 1989

From the beach, climb WI2+ for approximately
30m to the base of the first curtain, which is
3-4m in height and hollow behind. Sometimes it
may just be a short and small free-hanging dagger.
Whatever you encounter here it will undoubtedly
have little-to-no protection and possibly require
mixed moves to get up and over to the bench
above. The second curtain is about twice the
height of the first with slightly better protection
options. The height of the third curtain is about
5-6m and is typically much fatter than the second
curtain. A short section of moderate WI2 lands
you at the top of the route. | **Approach:** Located
just after a small bluff outcropping approximately
0.5 miles from the base of *Close to Home*; this
route is easily distinguished by three curtains of
ice separated by moderate ice benches in-between.
| **Descent:** Rappel via vegetation (top of the
bluff) or V-thread.

3. Redline WI5

70m
Bill McKenna & Steve Stauber, 1991

If you are looking for a difficult and pumpy lead, this is the route for you. From the beach, climb moderate-angled ice for approximately 15m to a short, vertical curtain with a bench above. Depending on the length of your rope, it might be a good idea to bring the belayer up to the bench. From the bench, climb a 45m vertical curtain to the top of the bluff. It should be noted that this entire route has sun exposure that will alter the ice in a matter of minutes. | **Approach:** From the base of *Close to Home*, walk the beach west (away from Homer) approximately 0.3 miles. You'll know you are at this route when you see the straight-up, vertical curtain from just above the high watermark to the top of the bluff. Access from the top may also be possible by climbing a nearby route and then walking the bluff to the top of *Redline*; however, doing so likely requires crossing private property, which it is strongly discouraged. | **Descent:** Rappel via vegetation from the top of the route or V-thread from mid-route.

4. Dog Day WI4

90m
Jim Sweeney & Billy Day, 1989

When conditions are good, this route is typically wide and thick from the beach to the top of the bluff, and provides everything from WI2 to a short section of WI4+. From the beach, climb 5m of WI2 to a 40m curtain of WI3+. A large eye-bolt anchor pounded into the soils can sometimes be found at the top of this curtain, making it a good location to bring up the belayer. From the anchor, climb a 30m curtain of nearly vertical ice, followed by a bench with moderate ice and mixed then the top of the bluff. | **Approach:** From the base of *Close to Home*, walk the beach west (away from Homer) for 0.2 miles. Not included in this book, but another route named *Creme Puff* (WI2+) is found just a bit more to the east, past *Granola Cruncher*. | **Descent:** Rappel the route via vegetation (top of bluff), V-thread and/or anchor if it can be found.

The shining sun is a beautiful sight ,but is often a bad sign for these climbs. When the temperature warms, they will start to fall away from the cliff.

(Courtesy Andrew Holman)

(Courtesy Andrew Holman)

(Courtesy Chris Walden)

5. Close to Home   WI3

60m
Jim Sweeney & Billy Day, 1987

A small drainage / creek swale from the roads and properties above creates this route in a large alcove. When accessing the beach via rappel, this route is on descent-left and is typically one of the larger ice formations in the area, which makes it great for toprope parties, so long as you watch for others rappelling from above. Also, snice can be abundant on this route, so it's encouraged to make sure your placements and protection are solid. From the beach, hike frozen terrain or ice for approximately 30-40m to a point in which you feel ice tools are required. From here, climb moderate-angle ice for another 15m followed by a short vertical section. Another short section of moderate ice (or mixed climbing) puts you at the top of the cliff wall. | **Approach:** Park at the very end of Saltwater Drive, then walk about halfway back to the highway; turn right and walk a creek / drainage swale through the alders to the edge of bluff. | **Descent:** Rappel from vegetation to the beach below.

6. Granola Cruncher   WI3

45m
Jim Sweeney, 1988

From the beach, hike a steep gully for approximately 45m to the base of the route. It's recommended you put your crampons on before making this hike. Climb about 10-15m of moderately-angled ice to a bench, followed by another similar curtain to a second bench, followed by small vertical curtain to the top of the bluff. There is another route that can be seen in the picture to the right of *Granola Cruncher* called *Creme Puff,* and goes at the same height and difficulty. | **Approach:** This is the first route on the left and approximately 0.1 miles from the bottom of *Close to Home* when walking east (towards Homer). It's typically higher up on the bluff and may require hiking moderately steep terrain to access the base of the ice. | **Descent:** To get back to the beach, rappel the route from vegetation at the top of bluff. If your ropes are not long enough you may need to rappel via V-thread from the base of the route, or downclimb back to the beach.

217

GLOSSARY

Abalakov Thread
a type of abseiling point used especially in winter and ice climbing. Also known as **V-thread**.

Aid
direct aid climbing, i.e., climbing a pitch by hanging from equipment that has been placed in or on the rock.

Alcove
a belay ledge that is surrounded on all sides by vertical rock.

Arete
the outside corner of rock or ice.

Black Ice
very old ice that has been mixed with scree and gravel. Or ice covering the road that is clear and hard to see until your flying off it.

Bolts
metal pieces that are placed into holes that are drilled into the rock, usually include a hanger as well. Can induce high emotions in grumpy climbers

Buttress
a very steep arete on the face of a mountain.

Chimney
either a steep, narrow chute with parallel walls, or a wide crack that the climber can fit into.

Chocks
rock protection that is wedged into cracks by hand. Nuts is a synonym.

Chockstones
rocks that are wedged into cracks, either by nature or by a desperate leader who doesn't have any other protection left.

Chute
this is usually steeper than a gully, and may be subject to rockfall.

Cirque
a deep recess in a mountain; it resembles an amphitheater with steep walls.

Col
a steep, high pass.

Corn Snow
unconsolidated granular snow that has gone through a short freeze-and-thaw process.

Couloir
a steep chute, which may have snow or ice.

Crack
the separation of two rock faces, ranging in size from the width of a chimney to microscopically narrow.

Crest
very top of a ridge or arete.

Dihedral
the junction of two planes of rock; in other words, an inside corner. The corner can be either acute or obtuse, and can face right or left. Also called an open book.

Downclimb
to descend by climbing downward.

Face
the sides of a mountain, a slope being more gentle (less steep) than a face.

Firn
consolidated granular snow left over from the previous year. Closer to ice than snow in density, it may require the use of crampons. A podcast by Evan Phillips (Firn Line).

First Ascent (FA)
the first successful completion of a route.

Flakes
long, narrow horns, or a huge rock slab leaning against a cliff. The sides of such a slab may form dihedrals.

Flared
a crack or chimney whose sides are not parallel, but instead form two converging planes of rock.

Free
free climbing; i.e., doing a climb or pitch without resorting to aid.

Gully
this usually refers to a wide, shallow ravine on a mountainside.

Headwall
where the face of a mountain steepens dramatically.

Lead
see **Pitch**.

Mixed Climbing
either a combination of free and aid climbing; or a combination of rock, snow, and ice climbing.

Moat
the gap between snow and ice and a rock wall.

Munge
dirt and vegetation that fills a crack.

Nailing
an ancient term used to describe direct-aid climbing with pitons.

Neve
consolidated granular snow. This is common on glaciers and snowfields during the height of summer.

Notch
a small col.

Nuts
see **Chocks**.

Off-width
a crack or chimney too wide to climb but too narrow to climb into. Usually something used to torture undesirable climbing partners.

Outside Corner
see **Rib**.

Overhang
a section of rock that exceeds the vertical.

Pass
the lowest or easiest crossing of a ridge.

Pitch or **Lead**
a section of a climb between belays.

Pillar
usually a formation of ice that is detached partially or fully from the wall behind.

Pitons
metal spikes that are hammered into cracks.

Ramp
an ascending ledge.

Rib
a short, small buttress. An outside corner is even smaller.

Ridge
a high divide extending out from a peak.

Roof
an overhang that forms a horizontal plane.

Runners
loops of nylon webbing that are threaded or looped around chockstones, flakes, horns, or chickenheads for protection. People who want to get into ice climbing but see the price of gear.

Saddle
a high pass that is not as steep as a col.

Screamer
a long and loud fall. A nylon webbing structure consisting of one large loop sewn in multiple places to make a shorter length. Used in places of dubious strength. The stitchings are sewn to be lower than breaking strength and tear as the climber falls. This reduces the shock of the fall on the anchor point. Screamer is a brand name of Yates Mountaineering.

Scree
small rocks that slide under the climber's feet.

Slope
see Face.

Spectre
pound in protection for thin ice and mixed lines

Spindrift
powdery snow blown off the mountain

Summit
the high point of a peak or top of a pass.

Swale
a low tract of land often wet or marshy.

Snice
not quite snow and not quite ice, something between the two

Talus
large blocks of rock, bigger than scree.

Tarn
a small lake.

Toe
the bottom of a buttress. What you'll lose if you climb ice long enough.

V-thread
a type of rappelling point used especially in winter and ice climbing. Also called **Abalakov** thread.

Zero Thread
built the same as a V-thread but with the rope threaded through the ice, leaving nothing behind. Save the planet, leave no trace.

Verglas
thin water ice on rock.

Fat City

ICE

Blue Ice

BLACK GOLD

AND

THANK YOU

Any project like this takes a substantial amount of help from the community. We have benefited from the assistance of some amazing people and knowledge of all those before us. We would like to take the opportunity to especially thank a few people, we apologize if we missed anyone and that is no fault but our own. We deeply appreciate all of you!

It goes without saying that there are many who came first to provide the motivation and spirit to help us continue this path of exploration. At times we were met with obstacles from those less inclined to share their wisdom. Fortunately those were outweighed by the likes of **Roger Pollard, Martin Martinez, Wayne Mushrush, Steve Davis, Mike Miller, Dave Lucey, Scott Mignery, Chris Roach, Paul Denkewalter, Tom Evans, Brian Teale, Ryan Shackleton, Joel Schihl, Eddie Phay, Cash Joyce, Ryan Johnson, Sam Johnson, Jon Cobb, Harry Hunt, Richard Baranow, Nick Weicht** and countless others. We hope this book stands as an example of what good comes from an inclusive community.

David Whitelaw, Steve Davis, & Roger Pollard (*Fat City and Urban Ice*) and the late **Andrew Embick, M.D.** (*Blue Ice and Black Gold*) for their excellent guidebooks, both published in 1989. These classics are excellent resources when they can be found.

Michael Meyers, and Travis Mcalpine require special mention for all of their assistance gathering information and helping us fill in the gaps in several areas of this book.

Chris Walden was instrumental in adding a few routes as well as double checking information. He also created the zero-thread how-to on page 13.

Charlie Sassara provided the history at the beginning of the book, adding an element that none of us could.

Lisa Delaney for her painstaking work at assisting in the editing of this book, as well as Kelsey's last two books.

Sarah K. Glaser for the incredible cover of this guidebook.

Photo Contributors:
Michael Meyers (*25, 60, 72, 73, 76, 78, 80, 81, 83, 86, 90, 91, 92, 93, 103, 104, 105, 108, 109, 128, 130, 142, 143, 145, 150, 152, 156, 158, 166, 167, 172, 173, 175, 187, 200*)
Chris Walden (*13, 161, 162, 168, 170, 174, 181, 198, 199, 201, 204, 206, 208, 209, 210, 211, 212, 214, 217*)
Zachary Sheldon (*176, 178, 180, 192*)
Matthew Tucker (*84, 138, 141, 215*)
Sherrie Soltis (*30, 72, 75, 160*)
Andrew Holman (*196, 202, 216*)
Josh Pickle (*157, 159, 160*)
Paul Guzenski (*11, 146, 149*)
Nathaniel Bannish (*26, 27, 98*)
James Brady (*14, 15, 19*)
Harry Hunt (*91, 144*)
Jordan Haffener (*115, 184*)
Thomas Tapp (*188, 190*)
Amber Johnson (*221*)
Ben Fisher (*164*)
Brady Deal (*22*)
David "Wildcard" Leon (*24*)
David Stevenson (*14*)
Joe Connolly (*141*)
Joe Stock (*27*)
John Borland (*96*)
Larry Nelson (*15*)
Niel Huddleston (*74*)
Richard Baranow (*69*)
Sam Volk (*89*)
Serina Marie (*10*)
Martin Martinez (*148*)

Advertisers:
AMH (*Front inside cover*)
Mooses Tooth (*Back inside cover*)
Cassin (*8,9*)
Xplore Guiding (*12*)
UAA Outdoor Recreation Program (*41*)
Hoarding Marmot (*54*)
Petzl (*64*)
Mountaineering Club of Alaska (*75*)
Alaska Guide (*195*)
Alaska Rock Gym (*Back cover*)

INDEX

The index includes each route from the book in alphabetical order. One important note on this section, is the GPS coordinates that we have listed in order to further increase your chances of finding a route. These coordinates may not be exact, and should be used in connection with the rest of the information in this book.

Route	Rating	Height	GPS	Page
Climb 4 - Victor Creek	WI3/4	50m	60.35703592, -149.340104	168
Climb 5 - Victor Creek	WI2+	60-100m	60.35712319, -149.3397147	168
Climb 6 - Victor Creek	WI3	30m	60.35696732, -149.335336	168
Close to Home	WI3	60m	59.64403218, -151.5901628	217
Clown Face	WI3+	25m	61.38247397, -148.5907022	122
Cool Runnings	WI3	300m	61.16963006, -146.3473435	194
Corkscrew	WI3	30m	61.35887663, -148.5746062	112
Curtain Call	WI3/4	25m	61.41137534, -148.8092903	105
Dance Party	WI3+	40m	61.38692509, -148.5942231	124
Death Lizard	WI2	62m	60.77996958, -148.8811219	48
Detention Hall	WI3	40m	61.35915533, -148.5746498	113
Dirty Harry	WI2/3	60m	61.27791636, -148.9811487	88
Dog Day	WI4	90m	59.644433, -151.600564	216
Double Take	WI5	50m	61.82878952, -147.6730182	157
Dragonfly	WI3+	50m	63.79530, -148.92400	207
Dreams of Brown Moose	WI4	130m	60.77297937, -148.8622798	53
Dr. Weiland's Evil Eye	WI6+	150m	61.16854571, -146.3474274	194
Easy Money	WI3	20m	61.0284648, -149.7547665	34
Easy Street	WI3	20m	61.01078934, -149.7016295	35
Eklutna Man	WI5	200m	61.270519, -148.980192	88
Emerald City	WI3+	140m	61.3799299, -148.5901414	121
Emerald City Right	WI4	140m	61.38036538, -148.5901472	121
Even Hookers Get the Blues	WI5/6	100m	61.06131631, -149.599844	26
Event Horizon	WI3	50m	61.52294991, -148.7088891	128
Eye of Opportunity	WI5	45m	61.38710353, -148.5944955	124
Fang Gully	WI2	90m	61.06380116, -145.9066344	186
Fate is the Hunter	WI3	37m	60.82596438, -148.9322746	45
Firing Line	WI4+	150m	60.76241437, -148.6755016	60
First Finger	WI3	55m	60.79002934, -148.904522	47
Fish Hatchery	WI4	80m	60.50497423, -149.418261	174
Flame Out	WI4	17m	60.9840718, -149.5979751	38
Flying Cloud	WI5+	110m	61.07013021, -145.896918	182
Follies	WI4	75m	60.78804029, -148.8481935	51
Fooligan	WI2	12m	61.069245, -145.896844	185
Fourth Stage Tear	WI5	70m	61.36298154, -148.578515	115
Fox Falls	WI3	35m	63.78100, -148.90300	206
Freak Street	WI2+	15m	61.01041449, -149.6999771	35
Freer's Tears	WI4	100m	61.26488513, -148.9962623	91
Fringe, The	WI3/4	68m	60.77367492, -148.8869684	49
Gingus	WI6	80m	60.77638101, -148.8902208	50
Glass Onion	WI5-	120m	61.06924568, -145.8964631	183
Goatsbeard	WI3	55m	61.37923822, -148.5896244	121
Granola Cruncher	WI3	45m	59.6438454, -151.5887865	217

Route	Rating	Height	GPS	Page
Gravel Creek Pillar	WI5+	55m	61.73590872, -147.9280417	145
Gutterboy	WI2+	30m	60.78737836, -148.8458177	52
Hall of Mirrors	WI3	20m	61.3822528, -148.5906166	122
Hands Across the Water	WI4	230m	60.77582066, -148.8050612	53
Hanging Tree Left	WI4	35m	61.09135405, -145.8907568	181
Hanging Tree Right	WI4	35m	61.09143885, -145.8907738	180
Happy Daze	WI3	30m	61.38727236, -148.5946996	125
Harry's Big Adventure	WI3	150m	61.41232072, -148.8101624	105
Hats Off to Herman	WI5	160m	61.25934583, -148.9773424	92
Have it Your Way	WI2	45m	61.19244963, -149.2584369	71
Headstone Pillars	WI5	180m	61.269642, -148.981467	89
Henry's	WI3	50m	61.49523591, -149.057462	99
Heritage Falls	WI2	110m	61.18410031, -149.2125416	74
Hillside Pillars Left Side	WI3	25m	61.74311761, -149.2193629	136
Hillside Pillars Main Falls	WI3+	30m	61.74311761, -149.2193629	137
Hollowhead	WI4+	100m	61.42488137, -148.8152484	102
Hollow Icicle	WI4+	100m	61.19112036, -149.2554664	69
Hooligan	WI2	25m	61.069320, -145.896889	184
Horsetail Falls - Valdez	WI3	80m	61.06754233, -145.906751	186
Horsetail Falls - Whittier	WI4	90m	60.76338706, -148.6771866	60
Hung Jury	WI4	55m	61.0641666, -145.9064581	186
Hypercard	WI4	40m	61.03031344, -149.7613544	32
Icicle Delight	WI3	12m	61.19270137, -149.2590867	72
Indecision	WI4	250m	60.82625163, -148.93259	44
Iron Curtain	WI4	200m	61.2882241, -148.981558	86
Jack Frost	WI3+	90m	61.37713015, -148.5887497	119
Jack River Falls	WI3/4	150m	63.31713944, -148.7001082	209
Jacuzzi	WI3	30m	60.35699192, -149.3352139	169
Joker	WI3	15m	61.38200272, -148.5904544	122
Juicy Route	WI4	85m	60.35689144, -149.3406728	167
Kantellia Falls	WI5	120m	61.83248128, -147.6660836	159
Keystone Greensteps	WI5	200m	61.06877412, -145.8971376	186
Kid's Corner	WI3	180m	61.80751532, -147.6928114	152
King's Beard	WI5+	70m	60.35684092, -149.3424601	167
Knifeblade	WI4+	35m	61.51239454, -148.740441	128
Lake View	WI4+	150m	61.35536748, -148.5739111	112
Landslide	WI3	60m	61.828885, -147.67254	157
Life After the Graveyard	WI3	30m	61.82866723, -147.6691544	158
Little Boy	WI2	25m	60.79025592, -148.9048317	48
Lost Chord	WI4	60m	61.41652879, -148.8173502	104
Lost Ice	WI3	60m	61.42215196, -148.8162219	103
Lost in Space	WI3	30m	61.42324695, -148.8195305	103
Lost World	WI4	120m	61.35619247, -148.5746395	112

Route	Rating	Height	GPS	Page
Road to Nowhere	WI5	240m	61.26840102, -148.9917345	90
Robopick	WI5	90m	61.83276705, -147.6649227	160
Sashimi Ice	WI2	200m	61.40658898, -148.8169554	108
Scales Left and Scales	WI2	10-20m	61.04332266, -149.7866616	30
Sea Wolf	WI4+	70m	59.6448753, -151.6072212	215
Secret Lover	WI2	77m	60.78073299, -148.8823703	48
Serenity Falls	WI4	200m	61.28936248, -148.9843451	86
Serpent's Venom	WI5	50m	61.37553571, -148.588147	119
Silver Haired Daddy	WI5+	120m	61.1684824, -146.3473938	195
Simple Twist of Fate	WI5-	75m	61.06938711, -145.8968951	183
Skin Game	WI4	74m	60.77387498, -148.8868618	49
Slim Jim	WI5	120m	61.41137534, -148.8092903	107
Snowball	WI2	80m	61.3727062, -148.5850989	118
Sociophobic Tendencies	WI4	350m	62.45160531, -143.1289724	199
Spaced	WI2/3	40m	61.82875301, -147.6732713	157
Split Finish	WI3	150m	61.4169335, -148.8158719	103
Spring Fling	WI4	350m	62.45342056, -143.1337295	199
Spruce Pitch	WI2	18m	61.19270817, -149.259533	72
Squeem	WI3/4	40m	61.4106034, -148.8089344	107
Stairway to Stardom	WI3	50m	61.91868872, -148.1163985	140
Starbright	WI4	130m	61.41137534, -148.8092903	107
STD	WI4-	30m	61.82886143, -147.6688728	158
Steamroller	WI4	60m	61.37172178, -148.5852331	118
Stratus	WI4-	25m	61.82701885, -147.6831976	154
Street Primate	WI2	20m	61.8238461, -147.6930848	154
Suburban Blues	WI2	60m	61.51210095, -148.7416956	128
Sucker Punch	WI3	180m	63.33477, -148.75573	208
Sudden Impact	WI3	25m	60.99974489, -149.6497626	36
Superstition	WI4	360m	61.943217, -148.0822336	140
Sword Fight	WI5	35m	61.36254864, -148.5779998	115
Sword in the Stone	WI6	70m	61.36029992, -148.5761556	115
Tallman	WI3	92m	60.7868288, -148.8418668	52
Taurine Scream	WI5	50m	61.86121659, -148.1942413	140
The Bight	WI3	35m	61.08894714, -145.8848528	181
The Corridor	WI4	650m	62.44621223, -143.1341235	203
The Last Frontier	WI4	25m	61.74641211, -147.8040251	148
The Nose	WI4	100m	61.269389, -148.981821	90
The Other Side of Life	WI4-	90m	61.37649818, -148.5886113	119
The Roaring Silence	WI4-	80m	61.37387051, -148.5865451	118
The Schoolroom	WI3	35m	61.35898452, -148.5746885	113
The Thag-O-Mizer	WI4	100m	61.83294038, -147.6638362	160
Three Amigos	WI4+	42m	61.38718304, -148.5945719	125
Three Ring Circus	WI3+	275m	61.19223346, -149.2620939	73

Kimberley Gray climbing her first pitch of ice while Marc Davis looks on

27